OPULENT NOSH

OPULENT NOSH

A
COOKBOOK FOR
AUDACIOUSAPPETITES

KEN ALBALA

THE UNIVERSITY OF ALABAMA PRESS
Tuscaloosa

The University of Alabama Press
Tuscaloosa, Alabama 35487–0380
uapress.ua.edu

The recipes in this book are intended to be followed as written by the author.
Results will vary.
Inquiries about reproducing material from this work should be addressed to
the University of Alabama Press.

Typeface: Minion Pro

Cover images: Photographs by Ken Albala
Cover design: Sandy Turner Jr.

The author gratefully acknowledges funds from the generous endowment
in honor of Tully Knoles at the University of the Pacific, which were used for
reproduction of color photographs.
Cataloging-in-Publication data is available from the Library of Congress.
ISBN: 978-0-8173-2188-8
E-ISBN: 978-0-8173-9491-2

Contents

Contents

Contents

Introduction

Nosh: derived from Yiddish nashn, meaning "to nibble," that is, to eat a little bit, outside of a regular mealtime, but sometimes in a quantity that might otherwise constitute an entire and even substantial meal. The attitude while noshing must be nonchalant, with an air of refined detachment, lest one be accused of planning to eat. One drops into an occasion to nosh, almost accidentally, and can thus be forgiven for overindulging. Noshing must not be confused with snacking, which implies purposeful eating, but simple and uncooked fare, usually out of a bag, though often quite satisfying. The nosh, in contrast, must be excellent food, cooked—and it can, if necessary, be leftovers eaten directly from the fridge.

This is a book for people who like to cook, and especially those who like to eat exquisite little dishes that are innovative and enticing. Cooking and eating should go together, like a horse and carriage. But the food industry has hijacked our hard-wired instinct to graze through the day by offering us "snack foods" that promise immediate satisfaction but deliver rather little in the way of true creative expression, or gastronomic frisson. This book is a clarion call to take back the kitchen, to devote a little time to devising exquisite "nibblies" (as I call them) that are exciting to make, have magnificent flavor, and contain excellent ingredients you choose yourself rather than a panoply of artificial enticements that enthrall the palate to serve the demands of corporate lucre. To put it another way: this is real food, beautiful to look at, delightful to consume, and satisfying in a way that no bag of chips can aspire to achieve. This is not mere snack food, to be consumed in a mindless, passive way.

Serious devotees of noshing will appreciate the small-format servings here, the élan of throwing together whatever happens to be in the fridge. Leftovers are paramount to the perfect quick bite. But some may be left wondering how to assemble such ingredients, what flavors meld best together, and what culinary repertoires one might draw from to achieve elegance, and indeed opulence. What to do with that jar of sumac, that unusual foodie gift you've been saving, or that technique you've always wanted to try? These are the questions answered here. This book is a guide to noshing with style, grace, and verve. The recipes included can be found here only. They are all the product of extensive tinkering in the kitchen over many years and provide a starting point for those who are anxious to begin a lifelong commitment to creating serious artistic nosherei. That is, precise and meticulously tested recipes are offered here simply as a springboard for you to dive into your own creative projects.

The glory of the nosh is that you can make these in the morning, late at night, or as a quick small meal. You can eat them on your own, or you can very easily double or triple the recipes to serve others. Noshing is universal, and there are no rules. The complexity depends only on the time and attention you are willing to devote, and the recipes here do range from very quick bites to more elaborate fantasies. But they all taste fabulous, and they are all unique mash-ups drawn from cuisines around the world. Everyone knows pizza and sandwiches, bagels and muffins, tacos and egg dishes—but mixed and matched, combined in unexpected and delightful new ways? That's the goal here, and if it tastes good, eat it.

WHY NOSH?

For the past century or more nutrition experts have been telling us that we need to eat three "square" meals a day for optimal health. They insisted that breakfast was the most important meal of the day, lunch must be taken on a midday break from work, and dinner should be the largest meal, eaten as a family at home in the evening. This structure was determined entirely by the capitalist work schedule and the middle-class fantasy of domestic felicity, which centered upon mealtimes. In reality it rarely worked out so neatly, And why should it have? If you think of our history as a species on this planet, we have mostly been hunter-gatherers, moving for much of the day, grazing, eating small meals that were punctuated by rare but large feasts after a fortuitous hunt. Our bodily systems can handle eating very little or nothing for long stretches as well as occasional glut, and we might even function better that way. I won't make any claims about how our Paleolithic ancestors ate, because in fact there was no regular pattern—and that's exactly my point. They ate everything they could get their hands on: vegetables, fruits, meats, and even grains and pulses taken from the wild. They ate these whenever they could, and the human diet differed greatly depending on locale. In the tropics people ate more fruit, and in the frozen North they lived on sea mammals and birds, and rarely saw a green plant. Once again, that's my point. We can and did live on extremely divergent diets. There is no one set of foods we are supposed to eat, and no particular time or quantity.

So why not embrace this irregularity? I think many people already do. We have been told that the breakdown of the family meal would be the demise of civilization. But still people grab food on the go, snack through the day, and eat a "proper" meal when it's convenient, but not as a rule. And for many cultures, this has always been the way they ate. Doesn't it seem strange that we are expected to eat at set mealtimes whether or not we're hungry? And that certain foods are considered appropriate for the morning, and completely different foods for other times? Eggs are for breakfast, sandwiches for lunch, a hunk of meat and potatoes with a side vegetable for dinner. Why? These may be convenient for economic reasons—carrying your steak to work and eating it at optimal temperature might pose logistical problems. But around the world there are no such rules. People may eat leftovers for breakfast, or consume their biggest meal at midday, as was the case for many centuries in the West.

Some people like regularity, and especially the way set mealtimes structure the course of the day. But this is a cultural phenomenon, not a biological one. Just imagine if our work schedules were more free, if people didn't commute, but worked when they liked and ate when they liked. We have just performed this experiment during the COVID-19 pandemic, and although my knowledge of it is haphazard and anecdotal, many people have told me that, as dreadful as it all was, being stuck at home during the epidemic was weirdly liberating, at least in terms of meals. Noshing, it turns out, is perfectly fine, even if some people may tend to eat too much. The fridge does call through the day. Perhaps a small nosh would be better than a full meal.

In any case, I do not advocate snacking mindlessly or grabbing little bits of prepackaged food all day. The recipes here are all cooked, though small in scale. They are also the best foods on earth, things that have no strong associations with particular meals. Thus, they can happily be prepared at any time of day, and most are fairly quick and easy, too. Even those that take longer to prepare are designed to be eaten through the week, like a freshly baked bread. The ultimate goal is not necessarily better health, even if that could be defined for all people. Rather, I aim to offer ideas for how to make good food that will nourish the body and soul, liberate you in the kitchen, and inspire you to eat really well, which I believe is among the most important things in life.

IS THIS FUSION?

I hesitate to call this "fusion cuisine." When I was young and learning to cook, "fusion" had already become a bad word. In the 1970s innovative chefs had been working to consciously combine ingredients and techniques from disparate culinary traditions in ways no one had ever seen before. By the 1980s, people were tired of it. The reaction to "fusion cuisine" was to search for the food that people actually ate, the undiscovered and underappreciated cuisines—in the words of the magazine *Saveur,* "a world of *authentic* cuisine." The implication was that playing with your food was phony and what readers wanted was something genuine. It also meant that hybrid cuisines (Italian American, Chinese American, Mexican American) were considered suspect, even bastardizations.

But if you think about it, all cuisines are the result of fusion at some point.

Are not our most hallowed culinary traditions the outcome of long and sometimes fortuitous evolution? Imagine the Italians saying, "Tomatoes from Mexico? Not on my spaghetti!" Sure, the pace of interchange has intensified dramatically nowadays. Mixing ingredients has become as easy as walking from one shelf of the supermarket to another. The masa harina and the Norwegian brunost are a mere fifty paces apart at my grocery. In the past it might have taken a hundred years for a new ingredient or technique to move from one locale to another—though there are examples of recipes having moved much more quickly. When the Portuguese arrived in Japan, for instance, the cakes and confections they brought were adopted immediately into the Japanese tea ceremony, and even after the Portuguese were kicked out, the confections remained, as they do today.

When tomatoes arrived in Italy, however, it was around a century before ordinary people began to eat them and another century until they appeared in cookbooks, but still they are in effect a slow kind of fusion of Mexican and Italian cuisines. This kind of fusion is inevitable and has happened throughout history as people have interacted through trade and conquest. It is a natural evolution, but nonetheless conscious and intentional.

Consider the example of medieval European cuisine, which enthusiastically adopted Asian spices and cooking techniques from the Middle East. Chefs knew that they were combining essentially different cuisines to create something new. It happened very quickly, and then a few centuries later, it went out of fashion. Some spices eventually disappeared—think of galangal or grains of paradise. Most were marginalized to a sweet dessert course, as was the fate of cinnamon, nutmeg, cloves, ginger, or cardamom. But other techniques and ingredients remained, such as pasta. This was natural culinary evolution.

Is fusion in the recent past or today somehow illegitimate because it's quicker or easier or has no lasting influence? I don't know whether we will be eating kosher Chinese food in the future or whether Korean tacos will survive. Those fusions happened because of the proximity of different peoples. But does that make the results any more authentic than putting together ingredients I find in proximity in my grocery store? Is the grocery an "unnatural" setting, while the streets of midtown Manhattan or Los Angeles are "real"? Is the strange juxtaposition of ingredients on a modernist menu just a silly trend, while everyone squirting sriracha on their burgers and fries is somehow more legitimate?

I contend that any ingredients that taste good together belong together. Keeping ingredients apart is kind of like claiming that people from different cultures shouldn't mix and that if they did, somehow their offspring would be illegitimate. For the same reason that people should mix as they see fit, so should all recipes, however their creators desire. Thus, the recipes here have been constructed not with wild abandon, but with serious consideration of how ingredients and techniques can happily meld in this global world that we inhabit.

A WORD ON SWEETNESS

Some people equate snacking with sweets. I am emphatically not against sugar or sweet things in general. In fact, I love hard candy. But I am of the opinion that sugar is best balanced with other basic flavors, an idea that stems ultimately from my work in historic cooking. In the late Middle Ages and Renaissance, it was not uncommon to use sugar in dishes as often as salt. Before that, people used honey. Most cuisines in the world include the sweetness of sugar along with sour, spicy, and savory flavors. And even in the United States we are happy with a sweet barbecue sauce, or ketchup on a burger. In this book, sweet flavors are always balanced with others.

Only in the Western culinary tradition—and more specifically, in French cuisine beginning in the seventeenth century—are sweet flavors banished to the end of the meal. Dessert, after the tablecloth has been removed, that is, deserted, is the only course that includes cakes and other sweets. Desserts usually consist of single-note sweet confections, completely unbalanced, or only combined with the flavor of butter. As much as the modern palate finds sugar on a chicken or pasta dish jarring, I find dessert simply uninteresting after a full meal, and most cakes just revolting.

Even more perplexing for me is sweetness first thing in the morning or as a snack. Breakfast cereal is nothing more than a vehicle for sugar, as are pastries, doughnuts, and most kinds of cake. Sugar was formerly an expensive commodity, but once it was produced on an industrial scale and became cheap, it insinuated itself into our snacks as a way to push more product, get people to buy and eat more. What we lost was the pleasure of cooking and the stimulation that comes from eating a dish with a full panoply of flavors. With this in mind, I hope it makes sense that I have omitted from this book practically everything that is simply a jolt of sugar. Cookies and cakes and such, which you can more easily buy if that's your vibe, can rarely be considered opulent, so for this reason "nosh" is defined here by its savory character. There's still plenty of sugar, but, again, it is balanced by salt and sour, which are worthy to be craved, and by heat and especially umami, which is perhaps an indispensable part of a truly satisfying snack.

A WORD ON RECIPE TESTING

The process of testing recipes and especially of using exact ingredients was something new to me in writing this book. All my life I have cooked intuitively, meaning I used a handful of this and a pinch of that. I cooked the way people always have, until fairly recent times. No recipe ever came out exactly the same twice, but I've been happy with that. With the exception of cakes and baked goods, which I don't like anyway, most recipes really don't need precise measurements. In fact, I often found myself here rounding to the nearest cup or teaspoon, when my habit of eyeballing would probably have given better results. Using standard modern recipe formats and measurements was a learning process for me. I even had to buy a set of measuring cups, though I balked at using a kitchen scale, against the common wisdom of chefs in professional kitchens, as I think it is a waste of time and energy and counter space. Cups and spoons are precise enough. Still, I think the effort has made for a better cookbook.

My intention is not that you will refer to my lists of ingredients and slavishly follow the way I made the recipes. Rather, I hope that you will use my instructions as a launchpad to make the dish as you like best—even departing radically from my way. In other words, I want you to learn how to cook for yourself, to be liberated in the kitchen. If I've done my job well, this book should become superfluous once you have the techniques down. You may have to refresh your memory now and then, and I keep hundreds of cookbooks around for that reason, but I almost never follow the recipes in them.

Think of it this way: if someone always uses a GPS navigation device to drive, they will probably never learn how to find their way around on their own. Should a road be blocked or the satellite go out, they are lost. It's the same in the kitchen. You should not need to have a cookbook by your side. You should be able to tell when a chicken is done by its color, and with a good poke, rather than having to trust a formula to calculate cooking time, or a meat thermometer, another tool I disavow.

Let me explain this turn of tactic. A friend had posted on a food blog that someone had been offered a contract by a publisher to write a commissioned cookbook on a very specific topic for a decent amount of money, in only a month. That seemed possible to me. Other people reading my comment to that effect immediately said I knew nothing about recipe testing, that it was impossible to do in that amount of time. And I found that they were right. I had never done formal testing. Instead, I cooked at least twice every day, until I knew how to deal with an ingredient or had mastered a technique, and then explained it in writing, using measurements only if really necessary. But I had never cooked a recipe several times, making sure all the moving parts fit together, tweaking temperature and cooking times, using precise amounts of salt, substituting ingredients to get the perfect flavor combinations. For this book I did precisely that.

The process created a lot of waste. My dogs were very happy. I don't think I had ever tasted food and spat it out before, but doing so has become a habit now. I had never cooked the same recipe several times in a row until I got it right. One dish here I cooked nine times. Most I cooked a few times, and when something came out perfectly the first time, it was usually because I'd already been cooking it for many years. Or it was just luck!

WHAT TO DRINK?

A nosh should never go down dry, as a rule. Even if you are pressed for time, lubricating the mouth and interior passages of the digestive tract should be considered indispensable. Naturally, the time of day will dictate the beverage of choice. For me, mornings demand caffeine, and afternoons scream for cocktails or wine, especially those tailor made to suit the nosh. Can there be opulence without alcohol? Perhaps, but I do not hope to find out.

There are those who love coffee—the brooding black sludge that offers a jolt of caffeine and leaves your mouth tasting like tar for the rest of the day. No amount of sugar or milk can diminish the assault on the taste buds made by a hot mug of coffee slurped as quickly as possible, plunging to the depths of the stomach not to gently arouse the senses but to shock them into a frenzied, jittery buzz. It may be the perfect drink for efficient cogs in the capitalist machine, pushing them to hurry out the door and get busy making money for their corporate overlords, who happily supply them with the swill all day.

Don't get me wrong, I love the idea of coffee. If I hear someone talking about it, I have to have some. In fact, the first thing I do on every trip to Italy is find a good espresso, knock it back, and then forget about it for the rest of the trip. I am also found drinking coffee in hotel rooms, and even when I know that the big urn of water for tea has once had coffee in it, leaving its acrid flavor forever etched into the metal. College dining service urns labeled "water" are as a rule always coffee-flavored. When in large cities or airports, I am swayed by the Starbucks on every corner, and unconsciously think, Look at all these people waiting in line, this has to be good stuff, I need some now. I pass a Starbucks every day on my regular walk to work, and now my daughter works there. Many times I've thought, I can just slip in and get a cup to sip . . . To tell the truth, as I write these words, I am conjuring up a deep craving for a cup of coffee.

But every time, I am disappointed. Years ago, I used to make a pot of Folgers or Chock Full O' Nuts in my Mr. Coffee machine every morning. I must have over-dosed, because I simply do not like coffee anymore, however often I drink it. I will concede that, in certain contexts, it is the only rational choice, and I do not hesistate to point out such instances in this book.

In contrast, consider the pleasures of tea, and you may understand my daily preference. It cleanses the palate, refreshes the senses, gently arouses the intellectual faculties. It expands the mind and inspires profound thoughts. Tea, paradoxically, both awakens you and calms you down. The caffeine somehow brings clarity and focus to the mind, keeping you alert but not stretching your nerves to a state of frenetic tension.

American tea is abysmal at best, designed really to be iced and sweetened. Good tea can come from China, its homeland, from Japan, India, and nowadays many other places. People who care about tea usually brew it loose, though I admit a big teabag of the sort the British use—without a string or a square cardboard tab—does make cleaning your teapot much easier. The best tea should be unadorned, but for a decent "cuppa," a half-teaspoon of unrefined sugar can be very pleasant. Putting milk or cream in tea is something I've never understood, though I respect those who insist, especially if you're drinking PG Tips or a comparably strong English tea. There is also nothing wrong with flavored tea, as long as it's not something like artificially scented hazelnut ripple fudge almond mocha. Earl Grey is a venerable flavor, based on oil of bergamot orange. Jasmine tea can be heavenly, and even a good smoky lapsang souchong is delightful. There is nothing as remarkable as a deep brown, almost muddy, fermented and aged pu-erh, the king of all teas, which can stand up to a nosh with backbone and fortitude.

I usually buy something like Taylors of Harrogate, a Scottish breakfast tea, or Barry's, an Irish brand. Two big bags and a pot of boiling water poured from the kettle into the teapot, steeped for about five minutes and perfect with just a little sugar. The most important part is not the tea itself but the cup I use, which I made myself in my basement pottery studio. It fits perfectly in my hand, and warms it without getting too hot. It's solid enough and shaped just right, with a bulbous base and tapered lip, so my hand never comes in contact with the hot surface as it does on a straight edged mug. The shape and texture of the cup force me to slow down. It inspires contemplation and reflection. So unlike a cardboard cup, whose dry edge you want to have in contact with your lips as little as possible, this is a cup that I want to linger with intimately. Of course, you can buy one that suits your own hand and disposition, but I insist that it should be made by human hands rather than by a machine. The difference is astounding.

What can be said of the sweet confections like a Frappuccino or fruity bubble tea, or even the latest thing to hit my city, a cheese tea, which has a creamy raft of salty cheese floating on top? These can be very alluring, but hardly suitable for pairing with a nosh. They're more like ice cream, a dessert, and probably taste best late in the day. Even a regular cappuccino doesn't sound that good in the morning, at least to me. Italians do it, but it worries them a lot.

Perhaps the more important question is: can alcohol be tolerated first thing in the morning? If you call it brunch, then of course people down Bloody Marys and mimosas. But we are not talking about brunch here, which in general I find a terrible idea, unless you have an entire afternoon to sleep it off and don't mind feeling dreadful the rest of the day. But how about a glass of champagne or Sekt, as served in Vienna? Not enough to make you blotto, but just enough to lift you up a little and make the meal more buoyant. I heartily approve. And don't go ruining your good champagne with orange juice. Use the cheapest stuff for that and serve it to those who like those flavors together.

In the afternoon, after work, or on a leisurely weekend, a good drink is the only responsible accompaniment for a great nosh. While this is not the place to hold forth on the glories of cocktails, let me entice you with a few choice reflections that might steer you in this direction. Choose your booze according to the season. It does make an enormous difference. In the summer, when you can hear the malaria-bearing mosquitos buzzing about your head, a good quinine-laced tonic with gin is the only sane possibility. A martini can be quite fetching, as long as you don't serve it in a classic martini glass, which will inevitably end up on your shirt. Rum is the drink of spring, with tart lime juice and plenty of ice. Or a Brazilian caipirinha made with cachaça. Even a rum and Coke, or Cuba libre, will be great. Only in fall can bourbon be considered, in perhaps an old fashioned, or better yet a boulevardier, which is bourbon and Campari and red vermouth in equal measure. Winter should be reserved for good cognac, neither mixed nor adulterated. I rarely indulge in such stuff now, though I was seriously spoiled in my youth. My father was given presents of excellent Hennessy X.O. and Courvoisier, and he didn't drink. So my friends and I regularly raided the liquor cabinet. Ah, those were the days. Where I live now, in California, it never gets cold enough to drink cognac. That's my excuse. But in its place I'll happily take good apple brandy, eau de vie, or grappa—all of which make really delightful cocktails that will go with the recipes here. Vodka, it has to be said, has no character whatsoever, which I guess sometimes you might want in a cocktail, perhaps with fresh juice (pomegranate or grapefruit is awfully nice).

On occasion you may decide to forego harder spirits and stick to wine. I thoroughly approve, and my choice for pairing here would be a bright sauvignon blanc, a pinot grigio, or a good dry rosé. These do not have to be expensive at all, and if you decide to throw in a few ice cubes, it actually brings out the aroma and makes it more appealing. For many of the dishes here I would chose sake, though, as strong as it can get, served cold in a small ceramic cup. And, of course, beer is always perfect with a snack. As I did with coffee, I think I had a bit too much of powerfully hoppy IPAs (India pale ales) when I was younger. Although I still like them, I think they can be rather too filling to consume in any respectable quantity. A cocktail is just more efficient.

A DISCOURSE ON TOAST

Toast will figure prominently in this book mostly because, as everyone knows, the sandwich is the perfect nosh. If you can get wonderful bread worth eating, I am of the opinion that it can only be improved by slicing and toasting. Toast can only be bested by proper grilling. Better yet, the apotheosis of bread is achieved by frying it in a pan with butter.

I will try to clarify some terminology here, because we say "grilled cheese," when in fact we mean shallow fried in a pan or flat-top griddle. Grilled cheese is rarely actually grilled. Grilled bread is brushed with olive oil and placed on a gas or charcoal grill—note that I hesitate to say "barbecue," a term that makes no sense in the context of bread. Equally confusing is the fact that toasting bread was originally done on a skewer or rotating metal contraption before an open flame and was considered a high art in days before the invention of the electric toaster. But that is more akin to roasting, before people started putting things in the oven and pretending it was a type of roasting, which it is not. Thus, I propose the following system of classification for species of sliced bread:

Simply sliced and uncooked. This is appropriate for room-temperature butter that can be spread, perhaps jam or peanut butter, and in a pinch mayonnaise-based salads such as tuna or egg in a sandwich (which are not salads in any real sense of that word). If you are feeling nostalgic, marshmallow fluff or Nutella may be a good choice. Softness is the major appeal, so this should be white bread, but it is almost always better toasted. That goes for peanut butter and jelly sandwiches and tuna sandwiches, too.

Toasted to a medium brown. While light toasting may be acceptable when you want both softness and a slight hint of the Maillard reaction, the true appeal of toast is its crunch and sturdiness. Burned toast is only fit for the garbage can. Pile on squishy toppings in the "open face" style. Soft pâté, spreadable cheese, even mayonnaise-based salads are often best on a single slice of toast, whether a long, thin diagonal slice of a baguette, a round slice from the side of a sourdough boule or even a rectangular loaf slice. Although this sounds willfully aberrant, in my youth I developed a preference for bread that was first toasted and then wrapped in plastic, and left to get soft and chewy while waiting for lunch break at school. I thought it only applied to white bread with tuna or peanut butter, but actually even a thick, crusted bread, toasted and wrapped, left to marinate, as it were, with ingredients that soak in, can be remarkably good. This is part of what makes a good submarine sandwich.

Grilled bread. A gas grill is the easiest, unless you have charcoal already going for something else. A ridged griddle pan on the stove can also work, but in any case you want dark grill marks and the smokiness a grill imparts. Brush both sides of a sturdy slice of bread with olive oil, sprinkle on salt and some dried herbs. Place on the grill at low heat and turn once when grill marks are apparent. For this, you can rub on a cut tomato for pa amb tomàquet. Or simply put a bit of salsa on top. Sliced avocado is sublime with a squirt of lime juice and salt. Obviously, anything you would normally put on toast is also great on grilled bread. Bare cold cuts on their own, or placed in a constructed sandwich, can be greatly improved by grilling, with a little cheese that melts on the grill, of course.

Shallow-fried bread. In this case I prefer not to place the freshly sliced bread directly into a pan with butter, because I think it soaks up a lot of grease before it gets toasty. Normally I will lightly toast the bread first, then put it into hot butter in the pan, as a sandwich or an open-face toasted rarebit or tuna melt. I then place it under the broiler for just a minute or so to melt and brown the top. I find that the bread never gets soggy this way, but instead becomes exquisitely crunchy and unctuous from cooking in the browned butter. You can, of course, simply spread butter on the toast and place it in a pan to cook. Or even, remarkably, you can use mayonnaise—it has an interesting zing when cooked into the toast. If none of this has impressed you so far, then fry your toast in bacon drippings, duck fat, or even beef drippings from a roast. This is so intensely flavorful that I almost hesitate to suggest it—unless you have leftover roast beef and some horseradish around.

Deep-fried bread. There are a few occasions when you will have a large pot of oil bubbling away and you will want to put slices of bread into it to completely deep-fry. The oil soaks in so thoroughly that the bread becomes an incidental vehicle for conveying grease to your mouth. With a proper English breakfast, it is indispensable, if deadly. A better use of this technique is to cut stale bread into cubes, heat your oil in a wok and toss the cubes until crunchy. Perfect croutons, which—although people usually use them to top salads—actually go well on a plate with eggs or other toppings.

Twice-baked bread. After you have sliced some bread, brushed it with oil or melted butter, and seasoned it, place it back in a low oven to get super-crispy and in the end not greasy at all. These should properly be called biscuits, twice-cooked. They make a fine type of toast for pimento cheese, chèvre, salmon mousse, or even a spread of sour cream and caviar. Yes, that's prime noshing!

Soaked toast. You've seen this done with a French dip sandwich or any kind containing gravy. Believe it or not, any toasted sandwich can be improved by drenching it in broth. In the past they called it sops—from which we get the word "soup," and "souper" or "supper." Jacobin sops, popular several hundred years ago, is one of my favorites: chicken and slices of cheese piled on toast in many layers, then soaked in broth. As an experiment sometime, take your grilled cheese and pour chicken stock over it, or even the tomato soup normally served on the side.

What not to do with bread. Never put bread in the microwave oven, under any circumstances. Never steam it, or it falls apart—though you can steam raw dough. I've heard of people steaming stale bread, but I think just grinding it up for breadcrumbs is a much better idea.

Can you make toast with a blowtorch, I hear you ask? Yes indeed is the answer, though it does pick up a faint aroma of propane or whatever fuel you are using.

Is there ever a compelling reason to squish bread? Yes there is: in fact, a tea sandwich can be made from thin slices of bread rolled with a pin until flat, spread with cold butter, and filled with cucumber, watercress, even sprouts. Remove the crusts, naturally. It's very delicate.

What about double-slicing bread? I do it all the time. Cut a thick slice of bread and toast it once. Then lay it flat on a board and slice it again horizontally with a sharp serrated bread knife, so you have two super-thin slices. Use as is, or turn the cut sides outward, toasted sides together, and toast again, so it is extremely crunchy. (You can't put both of the thin halves in the toaster on their own or the already toasted side will burn.)

Now, what if you happen to have a crummy toaster like mine, which sometimes on its own volition refuses to pop when the toast is perfect so that it begins to burn? Keep your nose in the air for just such situations. Run immediately to liberate the toast from its fiery shackles. If it hasn't completely blackened, you can resuscitate it by scraping gently but diligently with a steak knife over the sink. It will retain some burnt flavor without tasting adust. For reasons I don't quite remember, my mother called this "truck driver" toast. It was one of her specialties.

Last, the issue of buttering toast. I have, for my entire life, been obsessed with even and complete buttering of toast. That is, not a thin, half-hearted swipe that leaves half of the toast naked, or a wad so thick that you might as well just eat cold butter from the fridge and skip the toast. I demand a thin, melting layer of butter that goes out to every edge evenly, even if that take several minutes of meticulous knife work per slice. Do it haphazardly, and you might as well just not bother at all. The same goes for spreading mayo on toast.

TOAST

Octopus on Toast

Slice a firm sourdough baguette (see sourdough recipe) into a few long thin diagonals, and toast until brown. Spread on some feta cheese. It will want to crumble at first, but show it who's boss. Then take a frozen raw octopus tentacle and lay it on a wooden board so it doesn't roll. Using a sharp Chinese cleaver, and keeping your fingers well out of the way, slice the thinnest possible pieces from the octopus. It will be hard to do at first, but after a few slices, you'll get the knack. Lay these on top of the feta, overlapping them, and garnish with something extravagantly unusual. I found sea grapes in a jar in my local Cambodian grocery store. They are a kind of seaweed, in the genus *Caulerpa*, and do look like tiny strands of grapes, crunchy and briny. Microgreens or sprouts would also be lovely.

Octopus on Toast

Cinnamon Toast

We all ate it when we were young: a slice of white bread toasted, smeared with butter, and sprinkled with supermarket cinnamon and white sugar. It was satisfying, even when a little soggy in the middle, but really not something I wanted to eat as an adult. And then it dawned on me, why don't we have nutmeg toast? Nutmeg is a far more interesting spice. Or ginger toast? Better yet, why not get medieval with our toast? In my house that doesn't involve torture or pillage, it means a riot of spices with unrefined sugar. I like the combination of cubebs, which are resiny and hot and have a little spike on one end; long pepper, a relative of black pepper but more intense; and green cardamom (you remove the tiny seeds from the pods and use only the ones that are black and a little sticky—if they're light brown, they're stale). Then add freshly grated nutmeg, a few cloves, and, if you're feeling really adventuresome, grains of paradise, which come from the west coast of Africa. These can all be found with a few clicks online. Mix all those in equal parts, and then double that quantity with sugar. This is roughly what was called *pouldre fort* (strong powder) in the Middle Ages.

For bread, a good whole grain rye, thinly sliced and toasted, is fantastic. Spread with butter, sprinkle with spices, and then hit with a blowtorch, at a safe distance from the toast, lest it ignite and become adust. Or place under the broiler. The spices will be "hot i' th' mouth," as Shakespeare's Sir Toby would have said.

Beans on Toast

It doesn't sound fabulous. Though I've had it many times in Britain, straight from the Heinz can onto buttered toast, they have a much better way of doing this in Italy. Think of it as a kind of *fettunta* or *pan unto* as it used to be called. Sixteenth-century cookbook author Domenico Romoli became so associated with the dish that he was nicknamed Panunto. In its simplest form, it's just toasted bread with a sprinkle of salt and a drizzle of olive oil. Then put some good borlotti beans on top or, even better, zolfino beans from Tuscany, which are yellow and delicate. If you like, add some tomatoes, shavings of parmigiano reggiano, pine nuts, chopped parsley, and a few anchovies. A squirt of lemon, and you're good to go. Or, better yet, serve as you would Spanish tapas, with a glass of cold fino sherry. Now we are talking serious noshing.

Beans on Toast

NIBBLIES

I put these together not because of any inherent relationship among them, but because they're small, open-topped sandwiches that look rather like hors d'oeuvres but are actually perfect for a nosh when you have interesting ingredients in the house and don't want to think too much. Or rather, I should say, I didn't put any premeditation into these, but they taste very nice all the same. I will simply describe them, since the procedures are simple and quantities entirely up to you.

At a certain point I began buying *senbei*, large Japanese rice crackers, which are flavored with soy. They make a perfect canvas for an after-school snack if you're not inclined to cook. Lay down perhaps a layer of cheese to stick everything on, and then add anything or everything you can, arranging it all with a pair of tweezers if you must. The process of decorating each one meticulously is meditative, and I find it really relaxes me when I first get home after work, mix up a cocktail, and decorate a single, opulent cracker. You can also use shrimp chips, chicharrónes, basically anything that will work as a sturdy, crunchy base. The recipes below are a little more complicated, but as with my after-school snacks, you should feel free to decorate as elaborately as you please.

Shokupan with Halloumi and Broccoli

Shokupan with Halloumi and Broccoli

Get a long small loaf of shokupan (Japanese milk bread), and instead of cutting it like sandwich bread, cut a slice the long way, without the crust. Toast it. Then get a long slice of halloumi roughly the same shape, but a little smaller, and fry it gently in olive oil. In the same pan at the same time fry flat slices of broccoli. Spread some hot Chinese mustard on the bread and then top with the cheese and broccoli.

Nagaimo Latke with Kimchi and Smoked Trout

Take a nagaimo (Japanese mountain yam), peel it, and grate about 5 ounces. It will be very slimy, but don't worry. Heat a large pan, and add 2 tablespoons of olive oil. Put spoonfuls of the goop into the oil and flatten. When they hold together and begin to brown on one side, turn them over with a spatula. Remove and let drain on paper towels; sprinkle with salt. Add a dollop of mild kimchi to each. Then shred a little smoked trout, moisten with mayonnaise, and add a little to each latke.

Sweet Roll with Kamaboko Shreds, Walnut, Soy, Walnut Oil, and Kelp

Split a Hawaiian sweet roll. Shred some kamaboko (Japanese fish cake), surimi, or the like, and add crushed walnuts, walnut oil, and soy sauce. Place on each half-roll and top with fine gossamer shreds of kelp.

Pa Amb Tomàquet with Shredded Finocchiona Salami

For this you need a good sturdy bread. Cut a slice and toast it. Then rub gently with one stroke of a piece of raw garlic (too much overpowers it). Then rub vigorously with a cut half of a tomato. Add salt, drizzle with the best olive oil you have, and then top with finely shredded salami. The reason for that is so the topping doesn't slide off with each bite.

Soy Wraps

These wraps replicate nori wrappers for sushi but are colorful and very easy to use. I like to fill them with a little bit of raw fish like tuna or salmon, clover or radish sprouts, wasabi and pickled ginger, maybe a little umeboshi plum finely chopped, a little mayo, or a chili ponzu sauce. Sprinkle on shichimi togarashi if you like it spicy. I think these would also be fun to make with cold cuts, a slice of turkey and cheese, or roast beef.

Soy Wraps

SAUCES AND CONDIMENTS

You reach a point in life when you realize that a significant proportion of your refrigerator real estate space is devoted to condiments. This is the time to celebrate. It means that anything can be seasoned, perked up, garnished, or otherwise embellished into a spectacular dish. Condiments should not be a way to cover up an unpromising start, but still there is nothing sadder than a plain, unadorned sandwich, or a wan, gaping tortilla crying out for a dab of this or drizzle of that. Some contend that appropriate seasonings must come from the cuisine where they originate. So a salsa only belongs in Latin cuisines, soy in Asian, pesto in European. I could not disagree more, and much of the excitement of inventing new flavor combinations comes precisely from mixing and matching.

If I were counseling someone starting a new kitchen, I would insist on a permanent stock of several condiments and sauces. Many of them can and should be made from scratch from time to time, just for the sheer pleasure of doing so. But some are simply better out of a jar. Mayonnaise falls in this category, so does mustard usually. Ketchup, I will advise you from long and hard-won experience, should not be made at home. It can be, and certainly the process can be rewarding as a historical exercise. But the squeeze of the plastic bottle, now that the anticipation of the patting the bottom of the glass bottle is long gone, still beats homemade ketchup. The industrial product is simply a perfectly engineered food.

Those three are indispensable staples, and even though I rarely use ketchup on its own, it's essential for Russian dressing—equal parts mayo and ketchup—on which I think I could subsist. Further, no kitchen should be without at least half a dozen bottles of hot sauce. There must be tabasco: red, green, and smoky chipotle. But there must also be Cholula, sriracha, Louisiana, and probably a few others. They're all quite different.

Soy sauce and fish sauce are absolute necessities. I like the Kikkoman brand, but there are excellent and decidedly different Chinese soy sauces as well, and really fine Japanese types of all-soy shoyu if you can find them. Tiparos and Lucky are the common brands of fish sauce, but I swear by Red Boat. A shrimp paste is also good to keep around for making sauces. Korean gochujang and a dark and light miso paste must always be around. In my fridge there are also always a few little tubes of umeboshi plum paste, seaweed, Marmite, Vegemite, and other odds and ends that have half a shelf all to themselves. Don't forget larger jars of Branston Pickle, Indian lime pickles and mango pickles, and proper "pickle pickles," too.

Fresh horseradish is incomparable, but the jarred stuff works in a pinch. A little tube of wasabi paste I put in the same category, and it's made of horseradish too. The nose-burning effect of mustard is also key, and a good French Dijon mustard, a whole-grain German mustard, yellow French's (and brown Gulden's if you're from New York), must all be in the fridge. I'm not a huge fan of commercial barbecue sauce, but I always have a bottle around, Stubbs being a brand I think holds up for most uses. HP Sauce or A.1. Sauce is also very useful.

Always have tahini in the house, too. I'm not fond of bottled salsa, since fresh is easy to make as a pico de gallo, and tastes much better. But Chile Crunch brand, Laoganma Chili Spicy Chili Crisp, Fly By Jing, or anything similar, with garlic and chilies in oil—buy every variety you come across, they are all magical. My favorite is actually a Japanese brand (S&B) that's a little sweet, mild, and seriously can be put on any food on earth.

The dry seasonings should not be neglected either, and here I don't mean single spices or even spice mixes (which I almost never use). I mean dried ingredients that can be sprinkled on at the last minute. I have been a devotee of furikake as long as I can remember—any type. Seto fumi furikake, with seaweed, sesame, skipjack flakes, and egg, is my favorite. Shichimi togarashi the same: it's a complex mix of chili, orange peel, sesame, sansho (which is like a Sichuan pepper), ginger, and other ingredients. Tajín is great stuff, but beware, it's very addictive: once you start using it, it's very hard not to. The taste is sour and salty and a little spicy. It's perfectly balanced, on mango or just about anything. I also love my own fermented Meyer lemon powder—thanks to the tree in my backyard. It's a pain to make—salting for a year, then dehydrating and grinding. Not difficult, but it takes a lot of effort. Old Bay Seasoning—I know, a spice mix—I have also found really useful lately. In this same category we should not forget za'atar, garam masala, or even curry powder in a can. Sumac is also becoming easier to find and lends any nosh a burst of bright red pucker. Likewise, look for anardana (dried pomegranate seeds) and amchur (dried and powdered mango). Both are delightful, and I predict they will make their way into most groceries soon. Don't forget tamarind paste or fresh pods, another great source of sourness.

A cucumber pickle is probably the perfect addition to any sandwich, but it ought to be a true lacto-fermented fully sour cucumber, not some sweet vinegar-laden imitation. Naturally, pickled vegetables of all kinds are among the most exciting things you can use to enliven your cooking—sauerkraut descends from heaven late at night when everyone is asleep. Likewise, olives and capers should be on every table, pickled lupins too, which are heavenly. A few of these, a hunk of bread, and some cheese arguably make one of the best meals imaginable.

Behold two condiments, great to have on hand when you crave a burst of sour or sweet respectively. Toss them on a sandwich or bagel or into a stew; even a soup comes alive with a dollop of either. Please do not be alarmed that no measurement is required. I have never made these the same way twice, and it doesn't matter. The Meyer Lemon Relish is something like Moroccan pickled lemons, though I often don't add spices, which makes the relish more versatile. The charoset is the Sephardic version of the Passover thick spread meant as a reminder of the mortar Jews used to lay bricks while toiling in bondage in Egypt. It is very different from the Ashkenazi version, which uses apples, and which I deplore. As for the authenticity of the charoset, this is my own heritage, so I can do it however I please.

Meyer Lemon Relish

Slice Meyer lemons into a bowl, discarding the seeds. Make sure the lemons are not waxed; mine come right off the tree in my backyard. Pour on a generous amount of uniodized salt, about a handful for a pint jar's worth. Depending on the size of the lemons, that may be ten or more. Lay them in the jar, and then pour on more lemon juice until it comes to the top of the jar. You can add a cinnamon stick, a few cloves, star anise, or whole allspice. Just don't use ground spices, or the whole thing will become muddy. You want to subtly flavor the whole but be able to pluck them out later. Cover the jar and wait at least two or three months. The lemons get soft and jammy, and are perfect with chicken or fish. They will last a good year, but refrigerate once opened. I have also used just the peel, with the pith carefully removed, and it's great, if much more intense.

Charoset

Take roughly equal amounts of dried apricots, dates, raisins, prunes, figs, and any other dried fruit you like. White mulberries are great, as are cherries. Chop everything well. Pour red wine over the fruit to cover and add a good glug of honey. These you can also spice, but use ground cinnamon, nutmeg, ginger, or pepper. On occasion I will use grains of paradise (melegueta pepper) or cubebs, both of which are exquisitely fragrant and resiny. Once the dried fruits absorb the wine, start using the charoset, ideally on buttered matzo, but it really makes a great punctuation mark for any wan dish.

Nuoc Cham

I declare this the best quick sauce you can make, and I contend with equal conviction that it can be used anywhere and everywhere. It has to be made fresh, but it takes only a few minutes.

Chop a shallot finely. Juice an entire lime over it in a bowl. Chop a few small green bird's eye chilies. One is quite hot, two is probably enough. Then squirt in fish sauce, about the same amount as the lime juice. The cheaper versions are fine; Red Boat is fabulous. Then chop a few sprigs of cilantro and add that in. You can add a little palm sugar, too, though I like it better without. Use this to marinate chicken or pork or shellfish. It makes a great dip for wraps and a sauce for sandwiches of all kinds.

Dukkah

The first time I tasted dukkah was in Australia, where it had been popular a good two decades before it arrived in the United States. It seems to go perfectly with the shiraz wine that's made around Barossa in South Australia, or equally well with the zinfandel that's grown in my neck of the woods (northern California). Typically, it's eaten with a hunk of bread and good olive oil. But it's also great on a sandwich or as an all-around topping for anything where you want a good crunch. There is no reason to measure anything, and no strict rule about what goes in it. Try a handful of almonds, crushed, along with hazelnuts, some fennel seeds, sesame, some coriander, and cumin. The only thing that's key here is that you use a mortar and pestle to crush the ingredients, not a machine, which makes the crushed mixture too fine.

OPULENT NOSH

Eggs

Eggs are the quickest, easiest, and tastiest of foods to nosh on, whether pickled straight from the jar, fried in less than a minute, or mixed up and drizzled into a bowl of ramen. However, there is no subject over which greater disagreement is expressed than the cooking of eggs. Lilliputian wars have been fought to assert the correct end to open a soft-boiled egg. We all have an unshakable conviction that we alone understand the proper way to scramble an egg and trust no one else to do it. My father preferred his runny and wet, which I found disgusting as a child. My daughter insists that the eggs should contain milk and must be cooked slowly, constantly stirring, to incorporate the butter, so they come out soft and creamy. I will therefore not presume to tell you how to cook your eggs, nor will I insist that you really ought to do it my way, which I suspect some might consider overcooked and rubbery. Furthermore, no one needs me to tell them how to use the basic egg techniques: scrambling, frying, poaching, boiling. But I will show you many less common procedures, some from the past and a few devised for this book.

FRITTATAS

First, let's consider the frittata. Many consider it a lowly rustic cousin to the refined French omelet, but in fact it has a much older pedigree stretching back to ancient Rome. The cookbook attributed to the ancient gourmand Apicius contains many recipes that he called *patina*, which just means a flat dish bound by eggs. Actually, eggs went into dozens of his dishes, but the patina is really just a frittata, though for Apicius it allowed a much wider array of ingredients than nowadays. There was a patina of eggs, brains, and rose petals, for instance. I will spare you those with brains, but take a look at these two beauties (my translation):

> Another frittata of asparagus: Put asparagus trimmings that are thrown away into a mortar and pound, moisten with wine, and sieve. Grind pepper, lovage, green cilantro, savory, onion, wine, fish sauce, and oil; transfer the liquid to a greased casserole, and if you want, stir in egg on the fire so it thickens. Sprinkle with fine pepper.

Another frittata of elder, hot or cold. Take elderflowers and clean in boiling water, then dry in a colander. Oil a casserole and arrange the flowers with a little stick. Take six scruples of pepper [1 Tbs], moisten with fish sauce, and after you add the fish sauce, add 3 Tbs wine and 3 Tbs raisin wine. Grind. Then place 4 ounces of oil in the casserole, place it on hot coals [or the modern equivalent], and let it heat. When it's hot, break in six eggs, stir and thus thicken. When thickened, sprinkle pepper and serve.

Smoked Trout Frittata

With this ancient aesthetic in mind, try this patina of my own. You can use any kind of smoked fish; I just happened to have had trout on hand.

1 filet smoked trout (one side)
¼ C heavy cream
6 sprigs parsley, finely chopped
2 sprigs fresh thyme, stems removed
1 Tbs capers
Juice of ½ lemon
A few grinds pepper
2 jumbo eggs
1 Tbs butter

Remove the skin and any bones, then crumble the fish, moisten with the cream, and add the other ingredients, plus the herbs. You won't need to add salt. Stir well. Heat the butter in a pan. Pour in the mixture and let cook, covered, over low heat. This will take about 5 minutes or longer. Wait until the egg is set and slides easily in the pan. Then with a blowtorch or under the broiler, cook the top of the frittata until very lightly browned. Slide it onto a plate and serve. The texture will be very light and delicate.

Quick Frittata

Another very quick frittata, which will be easier to flip, is made with cheese.

2 eggs
1 oz mozzarella
⅛ tsp sea salt
2 slices prosciutto or other ham
1 Tbs butter

Mix the ingredients and pour into a hot pan in which the butter has been melted. Shake the pan after a minute or so, but don't stir. Eventually you'll feel the bottom slide, while the top will still be loose. Now, if you have the courage of your convictions (as Julia would have said), you flip it over through the air. Or, equally daring, you can slide it onto a plate, put the pan on top, and then flip the two together so the frittata goes from plate back into pan, with the uncooked side down. It looks impressive but is very easy. Cook just another minute, and slide back onto the plate to serve.

Quick Frittata

TAMAGO EGG WITH MI GORENG RAMEN AND YELLOWFIN TUNA

Sometimes, first thing in the morning, it makes perfect sense to fling open your cabinets and throw together the first things that urge to be cooked. Do not underestimate the power of proximity. If you buy good ingredients, if your larder is packed to the gills as mine usually is, you will inevitably align products that in waking hours seem incongruous. But now you're half awake, in that liminal time, neither dreaming nor fully conscious. The possibilities are endless because your hypercritical superego is still slumbering. Take flight.

My rational self would never have imagined this possible, but there was a can of yellowfin tuna in olive oil. There was a packet of Mi Goreng Flavored Instant Ramen that I had bought on a whim. The rectangular Japanese tamago pan was right below, at knee level. Even if you don't have these exact ingredients, I am certain this would be equally remarkable with regular tuna, ramen, and eggs.

1 small can Genova yellowfin tuna
1 Tbs Kewpie mayonnaise
1 pack instant ramen, Mi Goreng flavor
2 large eggs
Pinch of salt
1 tsp butter
Sprinkle of furikake

Bring a small pot of water to a boil. Open the tuna, drain and mix with the mayo. Boil the noodles and then drain. Mix with the flavoring packets in a bowl. These are meant to be used dry, not in soup, but I think any instant ramen would work just as well. Mix up the eggs with the salt. Melt the butter in a tamago pan. Pour in a thin layer of egg, top with some noodles and little bits of tuna. When set, roll up the egg and slide it all to the other side of the pan, and add more egg, noodles, and tuna, so the roll doubles in width. You should have enough for a third round and by this point you'll have what looks like a remarkably tidy omelet. Sprinkle with furikake and serve. It is soft and tender and, now that I think of it, reminds me distinctly of tuna noodle casserole, though that was never the intention.

MATZO BREI

There are two ways to make this traditional Jewish dish: either as a solid, leaden pancake or as light flaky nubbins saturated with egg. This is the latter, but fortified with a range of ingredients that on first sight seem incongruous, but which meld into a remarkably satisfying combination. It is anything but traditional, and it is *not* kosher.

1 ½ matzos
1 C milk
Pinch salt and pepper
2 eggs
1 Tbs capers
1 slice leftover turkey

1 tsp whole grain mustard
10 leaves fresh tarragon or
    other fresh herb
1 oz cheese such as mozzarella,
    Gruyère, or Havarti
1 Tbs butter

Break the matzo into small pieces in a bowl and cover with the milk. Allow to sit for a few minutes, and then pour off any excess milk. Add all the other ingredients, with the meat and cheese shredded finely. Fry gently in the butter, stirring constantly. The cheese will at first stick to the pan, but don't worry, it will eventually meld with the rest. You are looking for delicate pieces of matzo, just a little chewy, but not rubbery. That will take maybe 10 minutes on low heat. You can add a few drops of maple syrup if you like, but it doesn't need it.

Tamago Egg with Mi Goreng Ramen and Yellowfin Tuna

HUEVOS HAMINADOS

Everyone has heard that perfect hard-boiled eggs must be less than perfectly fresh, so that the shell comes off. This is true. Or that you should start them in boiling water. This is untrue. Go and try it, a few will always break. That's a price I am unwilling to pay. Above all else, you will be told that if you have a green ring around the yolk, you will be consigned to the bottommost rung of Dante's Inferno. So don't boil more than 7 or 8 minutes. This very traditional recipe scoffs at that malediction. Traditionally these eggs were roasted in hot ashes, as the name suggests. But I imagine that over time my Sephardic Jewish ancestors realized that this was very difficult in a small apartment and that you could get comparable results with very long, slow boiling. I have seen recipes that include onion skins or coffee grounds to accelerate browning. Then you have eggs that taste like onion or coffee. You need nothing but water and time.

Cook at least half a dozen, so you have eggs through the week. Start in cold water. Bring up to the boil and then lower to a gentle simmer. Leave them for 12–24 hours, adding more hot water as necessary, about every hour. Obviously, this is something you only make on a weekend when you're hanging around playing in the kitchen all day. Miraculously the egg proteins caramelize and become soft eventually. The flavor is nutty, almost smoky. The ideal way to eat the peeled egg is to flatten it between the palms of your hands, and sprinkle on some salt and a few drops of lemon juice. That's how my grandfather did it, and so do I. But here are a few other ways to use these eggs.

- Crush eggs with the back of a fork and mix with mayonnaise for egg salad, with a little chopped celery and a dash of Worcestershire sauce. On a slice of toast, magnificent.
- Slice the eggs in half and add to a bowl of ramen soup—it is much more interesting than a soft-boiled egg would be. It also adds a depth of flavor that complements either a pork- or dashi-based broth.
- As a variant on the Scotch egg, encase them in raw ground sausage meat and then dip in beaten egg and then breadcrumbs. You don't need to deep fry these, either—just fry in a little oil in a pan, turning them often until browned.

PANE PERDUTO

When I was in college in Washington, DC, my parents used to drive down to visit me and stay in a pleasant little hotel in Foggy Bottom. It was nothing extraordinary, but the breakfast was lovely. They had a French toast with apples, pecans, and a bourbony maple syrup that I replicated for many years as best I could. In the process, I learned that your French toast is only as good as the bread you start with, and the more eggs there are in the bread already, the more intense your "lost bread" will be later. It's also imperative that you let the bread go completely stale, so it can absorb more of the egg mixture. Equally important is that you let it absorb slowly, so you don't have a bready center, but a proper custard held in a matrix of bread. Challah is excellent, as is real brioche. But nothing comes close to panettone. I like to just cut a few wedges when I buy one around Christmas and leave them out for a few days until stale. There is nothing more to this recipe than mixing two eggs with about a quarter-cup of cream, a capful of vanilla extract, and a pinch of cinnamon. Dip the stale bread in and let it soak for about an hour, turning once or twice. Then fry it gently in butter. That's all. If you want syrup, go ahead. Apples, some toasted walnuts, whipped cream: go on and gild the lily if that's your pleasure.

Pane Perduto

If you want it simpler, then use this challah recipe.

CHALLAH

Although the bread trend of late has been a serious crust, large open holes, and an earthy crumb, this fluffy, delicate bread has inimitable charms. It transcends the ordinary by being abetted by eggs, butter, and a generous amount of saffron, which I believe is indispensable. But the most important thing is the honey, not only for sweetness, but also for structure and moisture. The technical word, I am told, is "hygroscopic," meaning the ability to absorb moisture.

> 1 Tbs yeast
> 1 C hot water
> ½ tsp sugar
> ¼ tsp saffron
> ½ C honey
> 1 egg
> 4 Tbs melted butter
> 4 C bread flour and more for kneading
> Another egg, for the glaze
> 2 Tbs sesame seeds

Proof the yeast with the water, sugar, and saffron. When frothy, add the eggs and butter, and begin to incorporate the flour. Knead vigorously on a well-floured board about 10 minutes. Let rise 1 hour, or longer if it's winter, in a floured bowl covered with a cloth. Then knock down the bread and stretch it into a long coil, rolling between your floured hands and twisting the coil. Cut this into 3 coils and continue stretching and pulling until you have three long, even strands. Braid these, and let the bread rise on a parchment paper–lined baking sheet covered with a cloth for 2 hours (or longer if it's cold in your kitchen), until the dough has doubled in size.

Heat your oven to 375°F, and brush the challah with beaten egg and sprinkle on the sesame seeds. Bake for about 20 minutes until light brown. To test for doneness, remove the bread and thump the bottom: if you don't hear a clear sound, or if the loaf is still floppy in the middle, lower the heat to 325°F and bake for another few minutes. Since every oven is different, you really need to be vigilant in watching, smelling, and poking the bread. I once baked this at 400°F for 12 minutes, and at 350°F for 35 minutes. Both attempts worked, but the resulting loaves had decidedly different textures. I prefer challah just barely baked through rather than overcooked and dry. This temperature splits the difference.

Let the challah rest and cool completely. Although you might think this dainty bread ought to be sliced, it is best to just tear off a hunk and eat it plain. It's also great smeared with butter, and then maybe jam. At a certain point you will decide to make thick slices, and then proceed with French toast—the best that can be made.

Or you can tear the bread into small pieces and let it dry out completely, and then proceed with the next recipe.

SAVORY BREAD PUDDING

This is a dish with ingredients that resolutely refuse to be measured, because the density, mass, and volume of stale bread pieces are impossible to quantify without extending into the realms of the absurd. Butter a casserole. Throw in your stale bread. Mix together eggs and milk, enough for the bread to soak up. Then mix in some ham (how much really doesn't matter), some cheese (likewise), and some kind of sweet vegetable. Red bell pepper is really nice, but so is leftover broccoli. Then bake it. About 350°F for 1 hour will do. You can cover it for the first 40 minutes or so, then uncover at the end to crisp the top, but even that doesn't matter much.

CRAB OMELET

The price of fresh crabmeat recently has placed it among the most expensive foods. I saw a small container for more than $40, and the price of a whole Dungeness crab was nearly as astronomical. Normally I don't buy canned crab, but I found a large can of blue swimmer crab in the refrigerator section of my local Cambodian grocery, and it was quite nice, if a little delicate. This recipe boosts the flavor just about as far as it will go.

1 Tbs butter	1 Tbs green tabasco sauce
1 C crabmeat	1 Tbs cilantro, chopped
1 shallot	½ C medium rice noodles
1 tbs ginger	2 eggs
½ small knob palm sugar	Pinch salt
1 Tbs fish sauce	¼ C alfalfa sprouts
2 tomatillos	

Heat the butter, and gently cook the crabmeat with the shallot, chopped, and ginger, peeled and diced. Grate in a little palm sugar and season with the fish sauce.

After it has cooked a few minutes, chop the tomatillos and add them, season with hot sauce as you like, and add the cilantro. Let any liquid cook off, and then add the cooked rice noodles and stir in well. Beat the eggs, add a little salt, and pour over the ingredients without stirring. Let cook until browned and crispy on the bottom and then flip over. Let the other side brown, and serve garnished with alfalfa sprouts (or another kind of sprouts). The flavor of this is perfectly balanced, with salty, sweet, savory, spicy, and sour. I dare you not to eat it with your fingers.

TIN CAN CASSEROLE

I woke around 3:00 a.m., as I often do, and immediately began to think about food. Eventually I became fixated on the idea of cooking in a can. Not with the contents of any can—this is no retro, 1950s dump-the-contents-of-cans kind of casserole, but rather layering ingredients in a can and baking them. A layer of rice on the bottom, then ham, cheese, corn, egg. The plan was to open one end, butter the inside well, form layers and then open the other end and press out a neat cylinder onto a plate. The first can I tried had a flip-top lid with an inner ridge, and nothing would slide out. The second couldn't be opened on the other end, so I ended up scooping out the contents. Delicious, but it needed a plan B. Finally, I took a biscuit cutter nestled into the tiniest cast-iron frying pan, copious quantities of butter and fingers crossed that I could get a crunchy tahdig-like bottom and soft melty insides. It worked. The fresh sage pulled everything together.

1 Tbs butter
4 Tbs cooked basmati rice
2 Tbs diced ham
2 Tbs raw sweet corn
2 Tbs soft cheese
3 or 4 leaves fresh sage, chopped finely
1 jumbo egg

Nestle your biscuit cutter in the tiny pan, and melt the butter. With a spoon, drizzle it along the interior of the ring. Add half the rice and press down with a long spoon. Then add the ham, corn cut from the cob, cheese broken in little bits, and the sage. There should be a half-inch or so of space left at the top. Let this cook over a low flame about 5 minutes to heat through. Then break the egg directly on top. It will take another 5 minutes or so for the white to barely become opaque, leaving the yolk runny. You can blast it with a blowtorch or put it under the broiler for a few seconds to speed up the process.

Remove the cutter from the pan and place on a plate. Carefully run a knife around the interior edge to loosen the contents from the side and gently slide out the little tower of a casserole. Sprinkle pepper on top, and eat while hot. The crunchy base contrasts so nicely with the gooey interior and runny yolk.

Tin Can Casserole

EGGS BENEDICT WITH ENGLISH MUFFINS

In the 1980s, after college, a few of my closest friends and I found ourselves back home living with our parents in New Jersey. I was working in publishing and making the long commute by bus into New York City. On Friday nights we would go out drinking in Freehold, which was the nearest thing resembling a town. There were a few little bars—Frebbles and The Court Jester—though sometimes we'd end up in Van's, a stuffy continental restaurant whose aesthetic catered mostly to the elderly. But they had a fabulous old piano player named Murray in the lounge. You'd just have to say, "In olden days a glimpse of stocking, blah blah blah," and he'd play it.

Inevitably, late at night we'd end up at the Manalapan Diner eating eggs Benedict and playing perverted mind-games—something like "truth or consequences." The late-night waitress was very tall, with an even taller blond bouffant hairdo and a slightly crooked mouth that should have had a cigarette dangling from it. She was obviously transported from the 1950s. We pretended that she couldn't hear the details of our heated conversations, though she clearly kept an ear perked, as was evidenced by a comment about prune danish one day. "Very good, you should try it." The eggs were perfect. On rare occasions when I try to make them now, I usually resist the urge to mess with the classic—well, except that the sauce is technically a Maltaise rather than Hollandaise, because it's made with orange juice.

English Muffins	Other Ingredients
1 C whole milk	1 thick slice ham
1 Tbs instant yeast	2 Tbs salted butter
1 Tbs sugar	Juice of ½ orange plus
1 jumbo egg	some grated peel
3 C flour	1 egg yolk
½ tsp salt	2 eggs
	Pepper

Heat the milk to body temperature, and add the yeast and sugar. When frothy, add the egg, flour, and salt. Knead for a few minutes until smooth and springy. Divide the dough into 6 balls and flatten each. Place on a piece of parchment paper to rise, about 2 hours. Then heat 2 nonstick pans over a medium-low flame and place 3 of the muffins in each, or whatever fits in your pan. Cook them, turning them over now and then, until brown on both sides, about 15 minutes. When you're ready to nosh, split one open with a fork and toast it.

Then place the ham in a skillet and just warm through. Heat water in a medium pot and place a metal bowl over it. It should be on a very low flame. Melt the butter in this double boiler set up. Add the orange juice, peel, and the egg yolk. Stir until thick but still runny, and set aside. In that same water, crack two eggs, just above the surface of the water. It will take just a few minutes for them to poach.

Now assemble the Bennies: muffin, ham, egg, and sauce. Plenty of pepper on top. Since you probably have no explicit memories of the diner, feel free to switch out ingredients. I think it's better with smoked salmon and wilted spinach. Actually, Anything Goes.

In that spirit, I offer you this variation. Substitute smoked duck breast for the ham, and instead of hollandaise, use this sauce:

1 poblano chili
2 Tbs hot melted butter
1 egg yolk
Juice 1 lime
Pinch salt

Place the chili over an open flame, and char on all sides. Place it in a paper bag for about 10 minutes until cool, then scrape off all the charred parts and remove the stem and seeds. Put the chili in a blender with all the other ingredients and whizz until smooth. Pour the sauce over your poached egg.

Eggs Benedict with English Muffins

CHAWANMUSHI IMPROVISATIONS

Chawanmushi is a kind of Japanese custard that many people think requires some remarkably complex technique. It's actually easier to make than a poached egg. Its appeal lies primarily in the soft, creamy texture, especially when contrasted with crunchy or chewy garnishes. In flavor it can be as delicate or as intense as you like in the morning, and is entirely dependent on the strength of the stock you use. The key to success, as I discovered after much travail, is adhering to a simple formula and precise timing, and after that you can use any ingredients you like. Here is a relatively classic version, though garnished according to my personal whim.

½ C dashi stock
1 jumbo egg
½ tsp mirin
½ tsp soy sauce
2 small pieces lightly salted salmon
A few wisps of dill
1 thin wedge of tomato
1 shiitake mushroom
1 tsp neutral oil, such as vegetable, corn, canola

If you can make dashi stock, by all means do. It is made with a handful of skip-jack tuna shavings (katsuobushi) and a piece of kombu, steeped in hot water and strained. You can also find dashi stock ingredients in tea bags; just try to avoid the jarred instant hondashi powder. Put 3 inches of water in a small pot, and bring to the boil. Break the egg gently into the room-temperature stock, and stir with your finger. On no account should you beat this mixture, or you'll have spongy scrambled eggs. Add the mirin and soy. With a small, fine-mesh sieve set over a small teacup, press the mixture through. This takes a few minutes, so be patient. Cover it tightly with tinfoil. Lower the heat of the water as low as it will go, and place the teacup in the pot and cover. Steam for exactly 12 minutes. If the water temperature exceeds 170°F, the liquid stock will be pressed out of suspension and you'll have wet scrambled eggs. Don't be tempted to turn the heat up or even peek at it.

Meanwhile, cook your mushroom in oil, and char the tomato, too, then set aside.

Remove the teacup from the pot and let rest 3 minutes. Remove the tinfoil, and arrange the garnishes on top. Serve at once with a spoon while still warm.

Now here's the best part: you can use absolutely any kind of stock and any garnishes you like. An intense mushroom stock was remarkable, with sour cream and chives and a few slices of truffle for extravagance. Chicken stock was amazing in custard form, especially contrasted with crunchy sweet corn fried in butter, with a few chewy chicken meatballs for garnish. A shellfish stock with shrimp would be so delightful, too. I leave this to your imagination.

Sandwiches

Sandwiches are the most serious subject for noshing. They should not be taken lightly. Nothing is worse than having subpar ingredients tossed carelessly between two slices of bread. The ingredients must be excellent, and the construction of the sandwich must be done with utmost concentration and can only be perfected with years of dedicated practice. I kid you not.

MONTE CRISTO

This is a venerable classic that somehow got forgotten in the shuffle into the twenty-first century. It's mostly a sandwich but behaves like French toast on the plate. The combination of sweet and savory is its real charm. Normally it's made with a soft, light brioche-type bread, but something sturdier gives it a little more heft and seriousness. I think a marbled rye is just right, or even pumpernickel. It doesn't really matter what kind of ham or cheese you put on, just keep in mind that the end product can never be greater than the sum of its parts if you use mediocre ingredients. But don't use an exquisite raw ham, such as prosciutto or speck, as it will be overwhelmed by the other flavors.

> 2 thin slices marbled rye bread
> 1 Tbs mayonnaise
> Generous sprinkle of Tajín or shichimi
> 2 slices of Gruyère or other good melting cheese
> 2 thin slices smoked ham
> 1 egg
> 2 Tbs buttermilk
> Pinch salt
> 1 Tbs butter

Spread the bread generously with mayo, and sprinkle with the extra zing of a flavoring powder. Add your cheese and ham perfectly flattened, not rolled or crumpled up. Put the sandwich together, cut in half, and soak each half in a mixture of the egg, salt, and buttermilk. Heat the butter in a small pan, just large enough to accommodate the sandwich, and when it begins to sing, add the halves, pressing down convincingly with a small spatula. Turn the heat down, and gently turn over the sandwich halves until the other side is nicely golden brown and the cheese melted. People will insist it be served as is, but if you choose to add a little powdered sugar or maple syrup, I won't complain.

Monte Cristo

SMOKED TROUT SANDWICH

The aroma of smoked fish strikes a powerfully resonant chord within the limbic brain—as if, the moment we transcended our habit of snagging a whole flopping fish from the riverbank and immediately gorging on it, we learned to nestle it over slowly smoking embers and then savor each morsel slowly. That flavor is seemingly hard-wired and should be considered crucial to our evolution. Those who smoked their fish destroyed potential pathogens, learned a method of preservation, and became fully human, leaving their bear-like progenitors behind. Smoke should be considered a primary flavor.

I have been told that, as an infant, my mother would prop me in a high chair with a hunk of oily, smoky whitefish to keep me happy and occupied for hours, and to this day I find it among the most comforting of foods. It is very difficult to find where I now live, though, so trout makes a fine substitute.

> 2 small square slices super-thin whole grain German rye
>   (Mestermacher brand)
> 1 filet smoked trout, skin and bones removed
> 1 Tbs or more mayonnaise
> 1 small tomato, chopped and lightly salted
> 1 clump cilantro, chopped

Toast the rye twice until very crisp. This type of bread is very dense and unrisen, and it becomes like a luscious cracker when toasted well. Tear the trout into strands with your fingers or a knife and fork. Add the mayonnaise and mix thoroughly. Spoon it evenly on the toast and top with the tomato and cilantro. Serve closed or open-face. This flavor combination is remarkably refined.

Smoked Trout Sandwich

TUNA MELT

Tuna is among the few perfect foods on earth, and this particular sandwich is the most sublime expression of its glorious flavor. Before we get to that, it is important to note that all tuna is not created equal, but you should never consider one type inferior to another. They are simply different species, though the labels on the cans are an attempt to dissimulate this fact. I was raised to believe that only solid, white albacore tuna in a can was worth buying, and only from one of the major brands—anything else was to be avoided. Not so. This kind of tuna is very much like chicken, white-meat "chicken of the sea." It's relatively flavorless and slightly dry, and will be dominated by mayonnaise for those who don't want a very fishy flavor. I always keep it in stock and do like it, but I have come to appreciate why there are many other types of tuna available.

If you venture downward in price, what is called "chunk light" tuna is skipjack tuna, another species altogether. It's darker and less coherent in the can, and its flavor is more intense—not a bad thing. Japanese tuna in a can usually contains MSG, but it is also very good packed in oil, and it is the same species, *Katsuwonus pelamis* (the Latin name comes directly from Japanese). It is not a bonito, as you may be told, but the same skipjack. This fish, smoked and dried, is the source of the diaphanous flakes of katsuobushi used to make dashi stock and miso soup.

If you search around, you might also find yellowfin tuna in a can; the Genova brand is always on my supermarket shelves, and it is really a different fish altogether, oilier and more forthright in flavor. More intense searching may turn up ventresca, or belly tuna. The Italians and Portuguese do an exquisite job with this, and the A's do Mar brand is about as good as it can get. But the Tonnino brand in glass jars is also lovely. Scout and Fishwife are two newer brands that are excellent. There are also brands of sustainable, line-caught, environmentally friendly tuna, and, though expensive, they are usually very good too. The Wild Planet mackerel is so good, you would be fooled into thinking it's tuna. The same is true of many brands of Japanese mackerel in a can.

If you can't find these, I suggest buying a filet of ahi tuna, cooking it very gently in a pan with oil, salt, and herbs, letting it cook, and pouring more olive oil over it. Pressure canning would be one way to keep this for a long term, but you can just put it in the fridge for a few days: it will be fine, and will cost about the same as the really high-end tuna mentioned.

Now to the sandwich: put your tuna, drained of oil or water, in a bowl. If you want to make homemade mayo from the oil, that's a great idea. Just whisk an egg yolk and lemon juice and drizzle in the oil. Don't worry if it doesn't get very thick, when you mix it with the tuna, it will be fine. However, Hellman's mayonnaise is great. So is Japanese Kewpie mayo in the weird squishy plastic bottle. Or Duke's, if you live in the South. Mix about 1 tablespoon of mayo into a single-serving tiny can of tuna, or two into a larger one.

Cut a generously thick slice from a large, round loaf of sourdough bread, cut that in half, and toast the halves. Then lay each half flat on a board and cut horizontally with a serrated knife, turning the half bread slice around as you saw with the knife, so that each piece is divided evenly along its meridian. You are opening the inside of the toast. Steam will issue from within. The point of this? There is no way you can cut bread thin enough and then toast it without it drying out completely and becoming too hard. This technique gets one side crispy, leaving the interior moist, with very thin sides whose volume won't completely overwhelm the sandwich. There's nothing worse than too much hard bread, especially if toasted, because it rips into the roof of your mouth. This makes a very thin sandwich.

Divide the tuna and mayo evenly on one side of the bread and shred some cheese on top. I usually use mozzarella. Sprinkle with a pleasantly sour dry condiment, which might be Tajín, furikake, or smoked paprika, whatever you like. Even chopped pickle or celery is excellent. Then place the other half-toast on top. Press down.

Heat 1 tablespoon of butter in a small pan, place the sandwich halves in the pan, with the cheese side facing downward and cook gently over low heat. Turn over after a few minutes, or when the first side is nicely browned. If you need more butter, add it. When the cheese and tuna are gooey, it's ready to serve. You have never tasted anything like this before.

REUBEN

There was a time when I was actively baking sourdough, curing meat, making cheese, pickling—all at the same time. It made perfect sense then to make sandwiches entirely of my own homemade ingredients. But unless you have these things in the works continuously, it's impractical to expect your quick sandwiches to be totally DIY. Nonetheless, I contend that if you can't get your hands on excellent ingredients, then making a few yourself does make an enormous difference in the final product. This is especially true of cold cuts, and none more so than pastrami.

If you buy pastrami at a deli counter, prepare to be disappointed. The same goes for a Reuben sandwich, unless you're at a bona fide Jewish deli (though not a kosher one, since a Reuben mixes milk and meat). Normally, a Reuben is made of highly spiced brisket, which has been brined, smoked, and then steamed. You can make it this traditional way, and it's remarkable. But there is another way. There is absolutely nothing traditional about this, but it takes little time, takes up very little space in your fridge, and makes one extraordinary sandwich.

Instead of brisket, start with steak. I used a well-marbled rib steak, sprinkled generously with salt, pepper, cayenne, cumin, coriander, and thyme—but your spice combination is up to you. I also added a tiny pinch of Insta Cure #1 to the mix, to get a bright-red color and that characteristic "corned" texture. Rub the steak well, put it in a sealable plastic bag, and leave it in the fridge for a week, turning every day or so.

Smoking is an indispensable step. For this you want a fairly cold smoke, around 150°F, which will be enough to gently cook the steak without drying it out. I used an oak log at the bottom of my old smoking contraption, got it started with a blow-torch, and then just let it smoke gently a few feet beneath the steak for about an hour. Apple or cherry would also be lovely. Oak tends to be too strong if you leave the meat in too long, so err on the side of less time if needed. Let the meat cool thoroughly, and then you can take one of two routes.

One is to slice the smoked meat directly and put it on your sandwich. It will be still quite rare on the inside, like a good steak. You'll have to trim off the thick edge of fat, since it won't have melted, but this is so delicious thinly sliced. If you like steak tartare, this is excellent chopped finely, too. The other route is to steam it gently for about half an hour. It retains its bright color and texture and flavor, and is ideal if you're only going to use a few slices at a time. You can also slip the slices into a soup, stir fry them, or actually use any way you would beef. But the Reuben is its greatest expression.

Rye bread is traditional, but if you can't get great rye, I suggest sourdough (see the recipe given here). The bread should be thinly sliced and gently toasted first. Slather both sides of the bread with Russian dressing (equal parts mayo and ketchup), then add a thin slice of cheese to each side. (I used Havarti with dill.) Then put a few slices of the beef on one side and a layer of sauerkraut (homemade is ideal) on the other, close the sandwich, and gently fry in melted butter, turning over a few times with a small spatula, until the bread is golden brown and the cheese melted. Serve with a real, lacto-fermented kosher dill pickle.

SOURDOUGH

I call for sourdough in many of these sandwiches, so I thought that a basic description of the technique would be fitting here. Making sourdough bread is more a state of mind than a precise recipe. If you think of your starter as a pet, and name it too, feeding it becomes a simple routine. And it is of course a living thing with its own moods. It may be very strong in some kinds of weather and then just tire out. And sometimes it just stops working or dies altogether. That's no big deal, because you can always make a new starter, it only takes two weeks. More important, you don't need anything but flour and water. The yeast and bacteria are already on the flour, on your hands and board, in the air. You just have to get them going.

People say a long-fermented dough is easier to digest; it's sort of pre-digested, and the bacteria are good for your gut. Depending on where you live, your dough may get very sour, but it might not. "Sourdough" is a bit of a misnomer, and sourness in the past was considered a fault in bread. Think of it more as a natural leaven—it's the way most bread was made before the advent of commercial yeast strains. Brewer's yeast, or barm, was also used in the past, but it gives you a very different, lighter kind of bread.

The method I have developed is different from most of those used today, mainly because I wanted to learn about how bread was made in the past. So I don't use a refrigerator. I also went so far as to grow wheat in my backyard, and ground it with a hand quern. I even built a wood-fired oven, too, making the bricks myself. Nowadays I use a conventional oven. If you bake once a week, you'll get into the rhythm and will always have good bread.

First, pour some flour into a large ceramic bowl that will house your starter. No, it doesn't matter how much—a cup is fine. Add water to make a thick batter. If your tap water is heavily chlorinated, use spring water. Then, next morning, add a half-cup or so more, and more water. Continue for two weeks. Leave the bowl on the counter, and you will never have to throw any of your starter away. Let it bubble. At a certain point it will smell like vomit, and you will be tempted to chuck it, but don't. It has not gone bad. This is a stage where the yeast and bacteria are learning to deal with each other. They will eventually settle down, the starter will probably get a little sour and will smell like good yogurt. After two weeks, name your starter. Love it and it will be a loyal companion.

To make bread, pour about one-third of your starter into another bowl. Add 1 cup of water and enough flour to make a firm dough. It will be about 3 cups, but please trust me, it doesn't need to be measured. You'll eventually be able to feel when the dough is perfectly hydrated. If it's a little wet and loose or a little more firm, it doesn't matter. The bread will be slightly different every time you bake, regardless of what you do.

Knead the bread a good 10 minutes. Let it rise about an hour and then knock it down, knead a little more, and form into a round ball. Place the ball in a willow brotform basket. Now let it rise, dust with flour, and cover with a cloth, about 12 hours when it's hot out, or even up to 24 hours in the winter. The longer you let it go, the better.

Then heat your oven to 500°F. If you have a baking stone, put it in while heating. I actually leave mine right on the rack. Gently turn the bread out of the basket onto a well-floured peel, so the spiral pattern created by the basket is facing up. There will be flour stuck to it, but don't worry. Slice open the top with a very sharp knife or lame (a kind of razor on a stick designed for this purpose)—I really like a star pattern. This is essential to let the bread rise up in baking rather than blow out the sides.

Slide the bread onto the baking stone. At this point I throw a few ice cubes into the bottom of the oven to create a lift. When the bread is nicely browned, slide the peel underneath and remove from the oven. Give the loaf a thump on the bottom; if it resonates, it's done. The baking time is very variable, so it really can't be precisely timed—but it will take more than half an hour.

Let the bread rest. If you cut into it too quickly, all the moisture escapes, and it comes out dry. Waiting even as long as a day is a good idea. To store, put your bread in a paper bag and put that into a plastic bag. It will be good for at least a week. If you have some left over when you're ready to bake again, just break it into small pieces and let it dry. Grind in a blender for the best breadcrumbs ever.

Keep feeding your starter, of course. And if you just aren't in the mood to bake, you can use some of the starter for pancakes or other quick-baked bread, and just keep feeding it as usual. Some people put theirs in the fridge, and I'm told it stays there happily. And if you go away for a long trip, just make a new starter when you return.

Now, if you don't have all this equipment, don't despair. None of it is essential. You can bake on a parchment-lined baking sheet, and snip the top of your bread with a pair of scissors. It will still be great bread.

MUFFULETTA

After trying several versions of this sandwich in New Orleans, I am convinced that there is no one standard and correct way to do it. The cold cuts inside varied considerably, as did the olive salad. Some were cold, some were heated; some a little too heavy on the raw garlic for my taste, some a little dry. All were excellent in their own way, but most suffered from an imbalance of ingredients. Either there was too much bread or too much filling. Too much oil or not enough. It was left to soak too long or not at all. I offer this version, not in any way to correct the venerable classic, but to scale it down for a nosh and give you an idea of how I like it, with a few observations on sandwich making in general.

In my opinion, a sandwich made of cold cuts should be equally proportioned between bread and fillings. That is not ⅓ bread to ⅓ filling to ⅓ bread again, but an equal 50–50 or 60–40 proportion, with a little more bread than filling. The bread should not overwhelm everything else. Nor should there be so much meat that the bread is an afterthought or mere vehicle for conveying meat to your mouth. Just as important, the sandwich cannot be so thick that you can't get it in your mouth. Open your mouth now. Measure it with a ruler. About 2 inches is a serious gape. Why would you make a sandwich thicker than that, unless you want to squish it and get it all over yourself? Have you ever seen someone actually eat a "Dagwood," piled impossibly high? Obviously, the thickness of bread varies, and the number of slices of meat you can put in depends on how thick your deli slices them. But if you follow 50–50 as a rough guide, the proportions will work. If that means cutting out some of the center of a bread, as it does here, then proceed doing so, and save the crumbs for another recipe.

Choosing the right bread for the sandwich is also of paramount importance. Muffuletta (or muffaletta) is the name of the bread in this case, originating in Sicily, but not something that can be easily found in the United States, outside of New Orleans. I think ciabatta makes a good substitute, as does a good long Italian bread. Where I used to live, in the Bronx, an Italian baker made a ring-shaped bread that I swear made the best sandwiches. A small round boule is my bread of choice now. In any case, the bread should have a crisp crust, essential to the soaking procedure that follows. I also toast it *before* assembly, to ensure that it holds up to the olive salad.

The soaking and pressing are also critical. Unlike most sandwiches, the muffuletta—and I should say, a proper sub also—is allowed to rest so the ingredients meld. (If you come from New Jersey, you will call this a *sub*; around Philadelphia, a *hoagie;* in New England, a *grinder;* or in New York, a *hero.*) The muffuletta is a distant cousin on round bread, but with similar Italian roots. You can make one whole sandwich and divide into quarters, or just a quarter. For a large version use four times the ingredients.

1 small round sourdough bread or your favorite bread
6 jalapeno-stuffed green olives
¼ C giardiniera (mix of pickled cauliflower, carrots, celery,
    pepperoncini, and red peppers)
3–4 Tbs olive oil
2 slices finocchiona salami (with fennel seeds)
1 slice capicola ("gabagool") ham, thinly sliced
1 slice mortadella
2 thin slices provolone

Cut a wedge from your round bread and then divide in two horizontally. Then cut out some of the interior so each half is of even thickness from edge to interior. Toast the bread lightly. Then chop the olives and pickled vegetables, and mix with the olive oil. Spoon the olive salad onto each half of the interior side of the toast, and then add layers of meat and cheese. Depending on the thickness of your cold cuts, you may want to use more or less of each ingredient. Just judge roughly the quantity that will be well proportioned to the bread.

Now carefully put the two halves together and wrap in tinfoil. Place a cutting board on top and pile on some heavy cans or the like. Let it sit undisturbed for 20–30 minutes. (If you leave it for an hour, it will turn to mush; 5 minutes, and the oil will not yet have soaked in.) A traditional version with a full, thick round of bread will take longer, but here the bread is thinner. The purpose is not only to moisten the bread, but also to allow the olive juices to permeate the meats and glue everything together. Freshly made, this sandwich would fall apart if eaten without pressing. But with a little coercion, the fillings join together joyously.

Now, if you want to approach this sandwich heretically, as I usually do, then along with the olive salad, pour on a little pomegranate molasses. Or drizzle with tahini sauce. Substitute hot Calabrian chilies in tomato sauce for the pickled vegetables. Any chili sauce will add a pleasant kick, if that's what you need to get you going.

Muffuletta

FISH CAKE SLIDER

Portuguese sweet bread is a fluffy pouf of doughy confection. It bears some relation to brioche, vaguely resembles good challah, and is faintly reminiscent of panettone. Like all these, it's light and squishy, and cries out to be pulled apart and eaten in little morsels. The Portuguese brought it to Hawaii, and the brand I find in California is described as Hawaiian. The Portuguese also brought it to Japan, where its descendants survive. Similar breads are found around the world, and I think their finest expression are the little sliders that make great sandwiches.

For this recipe you can start with fresh cod, haddock, or any firm, white-fleshed fish. Or you can simply buy little fried fish cakes in a Japanese or Korean shop. They're a little more chewy than the homemade version but just as good warmed up.

2 small Hawaiian sweet roll sliders
½ small cod filet or equivalent, about 3 oz
1 Tbs mung bean starch or cornstarch
2 tsp canola oil
2 large shiitake mushrooms, stems removed
4 leaves baby bok choi
2 Tbs garlic chives, chopped
2 slices Roma tomato
Drizzle of sesame oil
Drizzle of chili vinegar

Split the two rolls and very lightly toast them. Salt the fish generously and keep in the fridge for a day or two to firm up the flesh. Chop the fish as finely as you can, add the starch, and squeeze it repeatedly through your fingers. You're trying to get a smooth, amalgamated paste that holds together. Form two small patties, and fry them in the oil. Fry the mushrooms too, in the same pan, adding a little salt. Remove the patties and mushrooms after about 5 minutes, when golden brown. Chop the bok choi in fine ribbons. In the same pan fry the bok choi and chopped chives, for just a minute to soften. To assemble, put the vegetables on first, then the fish, mushroom, and tomato; sprinkle the other halves of bread with the sesame oil and the chili vinegar, and put the tops on.

Fish Cake Slider

OPEN-FACE SANDWICHES

An open-face sandwich should really be a fully extravagant meal in small format, piled on bread. Think of the Hot Brown of Louisville, with turkey and bacon and a rich Mornay sauce. Or the Welsh rarebit oozing with cheese. We're not talking of the elegantly spare and cold Scandinavian sandwiches, but hot gooey messes that you need a knife and fork to dig into. These are ideal for noshing, because if you have excellent leftovers on hand and access to a little toaster oven, they take just a few minutes. Here, I will simply describe a few combinations rather than offer an exacting recipe, because this is more about assembly than cooking. The only rule, I think, is that you should not use cold cuts. Wait for leftovers.

Roast Chicken

Start with your cold leftover roast chicken, about a handful. Remove the skin, and shred the meat. Add just a dab of mayonnaise to hold it together, and season with a little thyme and salt. Toast a large diagonally cut slice of Italian bread, about the size of your hand. Butter it. I know this sounds excessive, but it keeps the mayo from making the bread soggy, and it tastes great. Pile the chicken on the toast. Put on top some roasted, marinated cipolline onions. (You can buy these, but they are easy to make at home. Take a pile of the little flat onions and drop in boiling water a few minutes. Peel off the outer layer, and drizzle with olive oil, salt, and rosemary while still warm. Then grill them until lightly charred. Add more olive oil and some balsamic vinegar. Let marinate a day, and store in a jar in the fridge. Use them within a week or so.) On top of the onions, place some shredded young pecorino and a sprinkle of crushed rosemary. Put in the toaster oven for about 10 minutes at 350°F until the cheese is melted and bubbly.

Pan-Seared Salmon

Once again, leftovers: a handful of really good salmon, moistened with mayo. Put it on the same toasted and buttered bread. Then top with slivers of sun-dried tomatoes in oil. Really good Roma tomatoes dried in the sun and then covered in oil can be bought in a jar or made at home. People pretend not to like sun-dried tomatoes, because they were overused in the 1980s. I implore you to try them again. Crumble on some excellent blue cheese; Point Reyes is divine. Sprinkle with thyme, and bake in the oven until hot all the way through.

Opulent Pork Chop

Sometimes I make an extra pork chop just so I can have this sandwich for a nosh later. You want a shoulder chop with the bone, preferably breaded and fried. I do this by seasoning the chop with salt and pepper, dipping in egg, then dry bread crumbs, and then frying in a little olive oil. It keeps the meat moist and tender. When cold, cut it off the bone and slice thinly. Get your bread toasted and buttered, and add the slices of pork. On top add some mango chutney or, better yet, Branston Pickle. Then lay on a good sharp cheddar. Melt in the toaster.

SURIMI SALAD SLIDER

I'm not sure why we call surimi "imitation crab meat." It bears little resemblance to crab, but it's a delicious product in its own right. Maybe someday I'll start a campaign to rescue all the foods once claimed to be imitations of something else. Carob will be first on the list, then almond milk. Anyway, take it for what it is, a squished, starched, extruded fish product—usually pollack. I find the texture just as alluring as the flavor, and mayo really accentuates both.

    1 C surimi
    ½ C frozen peas
    1 small carrot, diced
    1 celery stalk, diced
    ¼ C Kewpie mayonnaise
    Splash of yuzu juice (or lime)
    Pinch of salt to taste
    4 Portuguese sweet roll sliders
    1 Tbs salted butter

Chop the surimi. Defrost the peas in the microwave for a minute and set aside to cool. Add the carrots and celery to the surimi. Add the mayo, yuzu, and salt, and then last fold in the peas gently. Cut each slider roll in half horizontally. Toast them lightly and butter them. This prevents them from going soggy. Spoon on the salad and put on the tops.

Surimi Salad Slider

TELERA MEATBALL SUB

Telera is a round bun used in Mexico to make the traditional sandwiches called tortas. It looks sort of like a hamburger bun, but it isn't soft and is a bit crunchy. I thought it would make a great Cuban-style sandwich, or Cubano. At that moment a few leftover meatballs were calling to me from the fridge, and this delightful snack was the result.

1 telera bun
4 small beef meatballs, cooked
½ C mozzarella
¼ C tomato sauce with basil
1 Tbs butter

Slice the bun horizontally and toast lightly, which is necessary to prevent it from getting mushy inside. Spread a thin layer of tomato sauce on the bottom half. Cut the meatballs in half and place them face down on the bottom bun. Tear the cheese into little pieces and place between the meatball halves and on top. Dab the rest of the sauce over the cheese and place the upper half of the bun on top. Melt the butter in a small, nonstick frying pan, and place the sandwich in the pan. Place a piece of tinfoil on top and then a heavy cast-iron skillet on top of the tinfoil to press the sandwich down. Cook on low heat, turning the sandwich over every now and then to make sure it doesn't burn and that it cooks through evenly. When the crust is browned and the cheese melted, cut in half and serve.

Telera Meatball Sub

KAISER ROLLS WITH PULLED PORK AND SLAW

If you grew up around New York City, you will be familiar with the kaiser roll, or hard roll. Its roots are Austrian, although I've never seen anything exactly like it there. It's a basic round roll but, as the name suggests, hard, with a distinctive shape—not scored with five slashes on top but flattened into a disk and then the five sides folded over, when risen forming a shape that resembles the imperial crown—and studded usually with poppy seeds, sometimes sesame. Sliced and topped with a generous slab of butter, they are carried by every bodega in the city. They are as quintessentially part of New York as the bagel. If you come from New Jersey, then you will also know that there are few things finer than a kaiser roll with mustard and a fried round of Taylor pork roll, or if you're from the northern part of the state, Taylor ham. In exile in California, I made do with leftover pulled pork and a red cabbage coleslaw, which is also quite fine.

1 Tbs dry yeast	3 C bread flour, plus more
1 tsp unrefined sugar	for kneading
1 C water at 110°F	1 tsp salt
1 jumbo egg	1 Tbs poppy seeds

Mix the yeast and sugar with the water, and wait about 5 minutes for foamy bubbles to rise. Beat the egg and add half to the yeast mixture; set the other half aside. Mix in the flour and salt gradually, and then knead vigorously 250 times. Kneading involves folding the dough in half, squishing as hard as you can with the palm of your hand, giving the dough a quarter turn and repeating. Keep the board lightly floured as you go. At the end you should have a smooth and firm dough. Cut into 5 equal parts. Roll each part between your hands vigorously so it forms a tight ball. Set these aside on a parchment-lined baking sheet for 2 hours until risen to twice their original size. Then heat the oven to 450°F. Brush the top of each with the remaining egg, and sprinkle on poppy seeds. You can also add a little salt. Slash each roll 5 times with a very sharp knife or cut with scissors, so you have a star pattern. Place in the oven, and throw a few ice cubes in to create steam. The rolls will be done in about 8–10 minutes. Remove them and let cool for a few minutes, shut off the oven, and then put them back in the oven for another 5 minutes to make them hard.

To make the pulled pork, get a pork shoulder roast, salt and season well with pepper, sage, cumin, mustard powder, and paprika, and place in the oven at 400°F for about 45 minutes until browned. Then move to a pot, cover halfway with water, and braise on low heat for an hour. You can then cut the pork into chunks or tear into shreds. Continue cooking, adding barbecue sauce and a splash of vinegar at the end, and keep warm on the stove.

To make the slaw, shred red cabbage until you have about 2 cups, and add a handful of golden raisins, 1 teaspoon of sugar, 1 teaspoon of salt, a quarter-cup of white vinegar, and enough mayonnaise until it just holds together—about a tablespoon. Put the pork on the sliced and toasted roll with the slaw.

HASSELBACK SANDWICHES

You've probably seen the Hasselback potato, sliced downward but not all the way through, and splayed slightly open when baked? They were invented in a restaurant in Sweden. Why not do the same thing to a roll and then stuff it with fillings? Surprisingly, the fillings stay put and it's very easy to eat. Slice perpendicular wedges out of a football-shaped roll, put in a toaster oven for a few minutes, and then butter the cuts, and toast again until browned. I filled the cuts with slices of pepperoni and cheese, and baked it until melted, but a tuna melt in this shape was astoundingly good too, especially topped with tomato.

Hasselback Sandwiches

BLT

I will not argue about preferences here, but let me just say that your bacon, lettuce, and tomato sandwich will only be as good as the ingredients you use. Out-of-season tomatoes, wan white bread, ordinary supermarket bacon—frankly, you can keep all that. But try thin slices of toasted sourdough; superior thick-cut bacon like Neuske's or Fall's, cooked in your cast-iron skillet slowly until just barely crunchy but with a little chew left; and then an interesting green like arugula or dandelion. The bitterness balances the sweet smokiness of the bacon perfectly. Anoint with mayonnaise. I do think the simpler, the better.

CUBANO

Like the BLT, this is a classic sandwich I nosh on often. The key to a good one is a light, torpedo-shaped bread, toasted, filled well but not overstuffed, and then cooked in a pan with butter and a tinfoil-covered brick on top, or some other heavy object. A cast-iron pan works well. As for filling, a few slices of roast pork are essential, but turkey is also very nice. A slice of ham, some melty cheese, and good, grainy mustard. Then just flatten it, and cook until it becomes a solid crunchy mass.

PIADINA

This is just an unleavened flatbread folded over ingredients like cold cuts, cheese, and tomatoes, a cousin to pita. It's found throughout the Romagna region of Italy and may even have been introduced when the Byzantines set up their Western capital in Ravenna in the sixth century. You can make piadina yourself with flour, water or milk, and a touch of lard for softness and flavor, or just use a flour tortilla, which is similar. You can heat it up in a pan for a few minutes to make the outside crispy and warm the cheese, or you can go completely over the top, as I have here with seven fishes. When I first made this, it was Christmas season, and I was thinking of the Italian American feast of the seven fishes, in smaller format. Use whatever fish you have on hand, preferably all prepared in different ways.

> 1 flat bread, such as a spinach burrito wrap
> 2 eggs
> ½ tsp sea salt
> 1 tsp butter
> 1 Tbs dried scallops
> 1 Tbs dried tiny shrimp
> 2 small marinated baby octopi
> 1 Tbs barbecued eel (unagi)
> 1 Tbs smoked trout

1 Tbs shredded kamaboko or surimi
2 small pieces pickled herring
1 small gherkin pickle
1 Tbs capers
3 chopped cherry tomatoes

2 Tbs clover sprouts
Sprinkle of Old Bay seasoning
1 Tbs of mayonnaise
Juice of ¼ lemon

Warm the flatbread over a gas jet on both sides until lightly browned. Putting it under a broiler works, too. Beat the 2 eggs with the salt. In a pan the same size as the bread, melt the butter and cook the egg over low heat, without stirring. Arrange all the other ingredients on the egg before it's set. Once cooked through, slide the egg onto the flatbread, and garnish with clover sprouts, Old Bay, some mayo, and lemon juice. You can just fold over before eating, or roll it up if you prefer the burrito shape.

Piadina

SUPER FRICO

The technique for this needs no more than a brief description. It is an expansion of the technique of frying grated parmesan into a flat, crunchy round. Start with 1 tablespoon or so in a hot pan with nothing else. Normally you would flip it over and let it get crisp and serve it with a glass of prosecco. Instead, add some thinly sliced and chopped pepperoni on top and flip that over. Then on the other side add some cooked greens, kale, or broccoli rabe, something with a little bitterness. Then on top, some ground sausage, and flip it over again. I stopped there and put it on a round of toast, but you could theoretically keep going with more layers, flipping over several more times.

Super Frico

Tipsy Trifle Sandwiches

TIPSY TRIFLE SANDWICHES

Sometimes I buy a kitchen gadget that seems to hide itself in the recesses of a drawer until one day I find it and put it to some use for which it was never intended. The rectangular sushi press was one such device. It can be wood or plastic. Basically it's just a rectangle open on both sides with a piece that fits inside to press down the seaweed and rice into a square shape. I thought, why not press a sandwich in it? And douse it with booze, just like a trifle. The first iteration was something you might easily serve in a restaurant—little squares of sweet bread with layers of cream cheese and crushed walnuts, with a layer of black currant jam in the middle. All flavored with rum and pressed tight. It was very much like a little finger trifle. What would happen with the same idea and savory ingredients? Behold:

4 thin slices long bread, cut to fit in a squared sushi press
1 tsp wasabi
2 thin slices raw swordfish
1 tsp salt

2 thin slices raw salmon
Sprigs fresh dill
2 oz blue cheese
2 Tbs vodka
Shiso leaves (available fresh at a Japanese grocery)

Put one layer of bread at the bottom of the sushi mold. Spread on the wasabi. Salt the swordfish slices generously and place on top of the bread, forming a distinct layer. Then add another slice of bread and proceed similarly with the salmon, topping with dill. Make the last layer with blue cheese, and add the last layer of bread. Sprinkle both open ends of the mold with the vodka and press firmly. Wrap tightly and place in the fridge for several hours. Then unmold and cut into squares. Serve on shiso (perilla) leaves, which are edible. These sandwiches are so dainty, and I imagine this technique would work wonderfully with any cold cut, cheese, or vegetable filling.

SALMON WAFFLE SANDWICH

"Waffling" is indeed a verb, though it has taken on a negative association implying prevarication, as if turning the waffle iron over from time to time were a mark of indecision. Exactly the opposite; it is a sign of confidence and control, carefully timing the cooking of your waffle until it is perfectly golden brown on both sides. Moreover, this verb should be used exclusively for cooking food in a waffle iron. "Honey, would it be okay if I waffled the pasta tonight?" "Here we come a-waffling among the leaves so green . . ." So I offer you this waffled sandwich, perfect in its simplicity.

2 slices white bread
1 Tbs cream cheese
1 tsp capers
½ C cooked salmon
1 tsp mayonnaise
1 Tbs salted butter

Lightly toast the bread, let cool briefly, and spread both sides with the cream cheese. Sprinkle on the capers. Then mix the salmon with the mayo. I used salmon I had salted two days and lightly smoked on the grill, but any leftover cooked salmon will work. Put the salmon on the bread, and press the sandwich together with conviction.

Then generously butter your cold waffle iron, put in the sandwich, and crush it closed. The sound will make you shudder, but don't be afraid. Now get to waffling, turning the iron over now and then over the burner on low heat. When it is browned and sizzling and the house begins to fill with the aethereal aroma of butter and fish, turn your waffle out onto a plate and dig in, with your hands.

CROISSANTS WITH HAM AND CHEESE

Everyone knows that the croissant is simply a vehicle for consuming obscene amounts of butter. It must be shatteringly crisp but also light and airy, and chewy inside, something rarely achieved by any store-bought version. Unless you have your own superb Parisian *boulangerie*, making them at home is the only option. But if there's one thing, perhaps the only thing, I have no patience for, it is the long and tedious process of lamination whereby the dough is rolled and folded, then rested in the fridge, then rolled again, and rested, and so on for what seems like an eternity. I ventured to see what would happen if I skipped all these meticulous steps. The results were delightful, though I admit, the trick of grating the butter I must have heard of somewhere.

1 tsp yeast
¼ C hot water
Pinch of sugar
¾ C bread flour and extra for dusting
1 stick salted butter (8 Tbs)

Proof the yeast in the hot water with just a pinch of sugar to get it started. When it's frothy, add the flour and knead to incorporate it. Let it rest just a few minutes, and then on a well-floured board roll it out into the thinnest square sheet possible. Grate about 2 tablespoons very cold butter with a microplane right on top. Fold in the four corners to completely cover the butter and roll out again. Feel free to flour your board again so it doesn't stick. Grate over 2 tablespoons of butter again, and then roll out again. Repeat once more. Cut the rolled-out dough into two triangles for two ordinary croissants or four for small ones. Cut a little notch in the long side of each triangle and stretch the other end so you have little Eiffel Tower shapes. Then roll them from the base up and curve them like a proper crescent. Put them on a baking sheet, and let them rise in a cool place for 2 hours. Then bake at 350°F for 30 minutes. Let cool.

Although the croissant really needs no adornment, I challenge anyone to resist ham and cheese with a good dollop of mustard, or turkey and avocado. As long as it's eaten immediately—there's nothing worse than a soggy croissant.

Bagels and Bialys

BASIC BAGELS

Here is a basic recipe to start. There are wildly complicated procedures out there with what I believe are extraneous ingredients. I've kept it quick and simple. No New York water, no malt, no blessing in Yiddish to help the dough rise. Well, the last couldn't hurt: *May Ihr zeyn gliklekh aun blyen* (May you be happy and prosper). This one begins like all the other basic yeast-risen bread recipes in this book.

> 1 Tbs instant yeast
> 1 tsp unrefined sugar
> 1 C water at 110°F
> 3 C flour
> 2 tsp sea salt
> 1 tsp olive oil
> 1 egg
> 2 Tbs sesame seeds

Pour the yeast into a large mixing bowl with the sugar and pour the water over, without stirring. In about 5 minutes it should be frothy. Add the flour 1 cup at a time, stirring. Then add the salt. Knead vigorously, with passion, for a good 10 minutes on a lightly floured wooden board. Fold over the bottom half and press down with the heel of your hand. Turn the dough clockwise, one quarter turn, and fold over the bottom and squish again. What you are doing is lining up long chains of glutenin and gliadin, the proteins that create air pockets in the dough. It will be a little sticky, but don't worry—if you knead quickly enough, it will eventually become springy and will easily come off the board. Clean the bowl you started with, oil it lightly, place the dough in it, and cover it with a dish towel. Let it rise for 45 minutes in a warm corner of the kitchen.

Then remove the dough, knead again for a few minutes, and roll it into a long coil. Cut that coil into six smaller coils and roll them vigorously until they are each about 8 inches long. They will want to bounce back, but let them know who's boss. Curl them into rounds, pressing together the ends. Leave them uncovered on your board for another 45 minutes, or until they have doubled in size. This will partly depend on the ambient temperature, so use your judgment—if it needs more or less time, that's fine.

About half an hour into that second rise, preheat your oven to 400°F and start a big pot of salted water boiling. Gently lift three of the bagels and drop them in the water for 30 seconds. Turn them over and boil another 30 seconds. With extreme care, using a large perforated spider or skimmer, remove them and set them gently on a parchment paper–lined baking sheet. Boil the next three bagels. While that's happening, brush the first three with egg wash and sprinkle with sesame seeds. Of course, you can use poppy, fennel, anything you like. Remove the other three and sprinkle the same way.

Place them immediately in the oven and bake for 23 minutes. They should be golden-brown but not dark. Let them cool, or if you can't wait, start stuffing them in your mouth the moment you can handle them.

To store them—only when completely cooled—place in a paper bag and put that into a plastic shopping bag. The paper bag will absorb excess moisture and will prevent mold from growing. If you want to freeze them, just a plastic bag is okay, but it makes more sense to wrap them individually in small zipped sandwich bags, sliced before you freeze them, and with the cut ends facing out, so you can separate them more easily and pop them in the toaster.

I do believe a toasted bagel is under most circumstances superior, unless they are utterly fresh. Even then, toasting enlivens them immeasurably.

EGG SALAD ON BAGEL

In Japan people seem to go wild over the tamago sando. The craze has spread to California and I'm sure elsewhere too. The tamago sando consists of two triangles or rectangles of crustless, poufy white bread, or shokupan, which bears a certain similarity to Wonder Bread in its industrial origins, but is even lighter and fluffier. The bread is buttered and contains a creamy egg salad spread that tastes a little sweet, and the Kewpie mayo is definitely laced with MSG. I've tried these at 7-Eleven, Lawsons, and FamilyMart, the three big *conbini,* or convenience stores, in Japan. The tamago sando is good on the run (or a long, aimless perambulation in my case), and it can be very satisfying. But every time I've tasted it, I think how great it might be on something more hefty, with a bit of contrasting crunch, some more oomph in seasoning. Hence the origin of this mash-up.

First, a word on store-bought bagels, should you prefer to purchase them. Outside the New York metropolitan area, which definitely includes my home state of New Jersey, there is nothing like a bagel. There are some interesting round breads. Sometimes they're even boiled. I've convinced myself that these mediocre excuses for a bagel are better than no bagels at all, but let me assure you, among the first things I do when I get to the city where I was born (Brooklyn, to be precise) is to find some bagels. There was a great shop on the Upper West Side a few blocks south of Columbia University—Happy Singing Bagels, or at least that's what I called it. Their cinnamon raisin bagels with lox spread were incredible. (Yes, I can hear you gasp—but sweetness and spice and smoky fish and creamy cheese do go together wonderfully. And no one there ever looked askance; many people ordered it.) There were great bagels in New Jersey, too, Eli's and then Bagel World in Manalapan, that were a staple every weekend when I was young. But I digress. Find the best bagel you can, or use the basic recipe above.

1 sesame bagel
2 eggs
Pinch of salt
2 Tbs Kewpie mayo
1 Tbs furikake
Sprinkle of shichimi togarashi

Cut the bagel in half horizontally and eviscerate slightly. This is not to save calories by removing bread, it's to keep the precise proportion of dough to filling and keep that filling in place. The bigger your bagel, the more you may need to remove. Just a few pinches will usually do—and be sure to save them for breadcrumbs. Toast the bagel halves, and set aside to cool.

Put the eggs in cold water to start, bring to the boil, and let boil gently for 7–10 minutes, depending on how you like them. Less than 7 minutes and the yolks will be too runny, more than 10 minutes and they will start to go greenish. That really doesn't bother me, so if you want to err on the side of well boiled, go ahead. But I do insist you not throw them cold from the fridge into boiling water as people seem to be doing lately. They will crack. Fresh eggs will be impossible to peel, so if they've been sitting in the fridge a week or longer, all the better. Run under cold water, tap them all around, and gently separate shell and inner membrane, again so the shell comes off easily. If it doesn't, it makes no difference at all because you're about to bash them up.

Bash the eggs into small bits using a fork, then add a small pinch of salt and two good squeezes of Kewpie mayo. Mix all together with the seaweed flakes. Pile the egg salad on the bagel halves and sprinkle with the togarashi. If this doesn't make you forget fluffy Japanese white bread, I don't know what will.

SMOKED TURKEY AND HAVARTI ON WHOLE WHEAT BAGEL

Sometimes flavors meld so perfectly and simply that you have to write down a recipe and remember it. This is one of those. The crunch of the sunflower seeds is essential.

1 whole wheat bagel
4 large shiitake mushrooms
1 tsp butter
Pinch of salt
Another 1 tsp butter
2 tsp dry roasted sunflower seeds
4 thin slices smoked turkey
2 slices caraway Havarti
½ avocado
Squeeze of lime juice

Cut the bagel in half horizontally, and pull out a little of the dough. This is not to save calories, but to create an even proportion of dough to toppings. Toast the bagel. Meanwhile, remove the stems from the mushrooms, then slice and fry the tops in 1 teaspoon butter with a pinch of salt. Then add a little more butter (another teaspoon) to the pan and fry the bagels face down until even crispier. Then put them face up on a plate and sprinkle with sunflower seeds. Add the turkey and cheese. Put into a toaster oven at 400°F for 5 minutes so the cheese melts. Slice the avocado, sprinkle with lime juice and salt, then put it on top of the melted cheese, and serve hot.

WELSH RABBITS ON BAGELS

It has been a long-running joke, since medieval times, that a Welshman cannot resist toasted cheese. There is even a story about why there are no Welshmen in heaven. God had gotten tired of listening to their language and incessant singing. So prankster St. Peter stood outside the pearly gates and yelled "toasted cheese!" and all the Welshmen ran out. Then he closed the gates behind them. It is unsurprising that this dish bears association with Wales. But why a rabbit, or lack of rabbit? The alternative name *rarebit* is apparently a corruption, and in any case makes even less sense. There are various ways to make this, and it is not just cheese melted on toast, but rather a kind of elevated cheese sauce made with beer and mustard. My daughter and I hiked around Wales and had a few really superb classic iterations, but here I've taken more than a few liberties with it. So maybe it should be renamed a Lower East Side Rabbit, Osaka Rabbit, or maybe a bagel fondue. I offer you three variations on a theme.

#1

1 pumpernickel bagel
1 slice thick-cut bacon
¼ small onion
½ tsp dried tarragon
1 tsp flour

½ tsp mustard powder
⅓–½ C milk
1½ oz extra-sharp cheddar
¹⁄₁₆ tsp (pinch) sodium citrate
2 Tbs rye whiskey

Slice the bagel in half horizontally, and eviscerate slightly to create a trough within. Toast the halves. Then chop the bacon into small batons and fry gently in a small nonstick pan until the fat is rendered and the bacon is crisp. Remove the bacon and set it on paper towels. Chop the onion finely and fry in the bacon fat, gently, about 5–10 minutes until browned, then add the tarragon and flour. Stir constantly for a few minutes to cook off the flour. Add the mustard powder, then add the milk, and continue stirring. Add the cheese and stir over medium heat until melted. You may need to add a little more milk if it thickens too quickly. Add the sodium citrate, which will prevent it from breaking. When melted and smooth, add the whiskey. Pour over the bagels and top with the bacon batons. Place under the broiler or in a toaster oven for a minute just to brown the top and keep it hot until ready to serve.

#2

1 pumpernickel bagel
1 tsp butter
1 tsp flour
⅓ C dashi stock
⅓ C dry sake

¹⁄₁₆ tsp (pinch) sodium citrate
1½ oz Gruyère cheese
½ sheet nori
1 Tbs tiny Japanese preserved
    clams (*asari no tsukudani*)

Slice, eviscerate, and toast the bagel as above. Melt the butter, add the flour, and stir over low heat for 2 minutes. Add the stock, sake, and sodium citrate. Then add the Gruyère and keep stirring until thickened. Crumble the nori into the melted cheese, then pour the mixture over the bagel. Top with preserved tiny clams or something similar, such as tiny anchovies. You can sometimes find this in a Japanese grocery, or pick some up on a trip to Japan. They're easily found in the covered shopping arcade in Kyoto. They are cooked in soy, sake, sugar, and ginger until sticky—and could probably be made at home, too, if you could find tiny clams.

#3

1 pumpernickel bagel	1 tsp flour
2 oz ground turkey	½ C sauvignon blanc, or
¼ tsp salt	more if necessary
¼ tsp dried basil	1/16 tsp (pinch) sodium citrate
¼ tsp paprika	2 oz cheese curds (squeaky cheese)
1 tsp olive oil	Sprinkle of Tajín seasoning
1 tsp butter	

Prepare the bagel as in nos. 1 and 2, above. Season the turkey and fry in the olive oil. Remove to a bowl. Add the butter and flour to the same pan, stirring over low heat for a few minutes. Add the wine, sodium citrate, and cheese curds. Let all melt and get smooth. Then pour the mixture over the bagel halves and top with the turkey. Sprinkle with the Tajín. Put under the broiler for a minute to brown the top.

Welsh Rabbits on Bagels

GRAVLAX ON BAGEL

When I was maybe eight or ten years old, my father and I would rent a rowboat on the Jersey shore and fish for flounder. There was a certain ritual to these outings. Waking up before the sun, piling the rods and tackle into his tiny, old blue four-door Corvair, getting donuts, and launching just before the sun came up. One rod in particular, I remember, my mother bought him for their anniversary—it was short and beige and had a silk line. This wasn't casting. You just put lead weights on the line and dropped it down. The flounders were on the bottom. We sometimes brought home a dozen good-sized fish.

How it came to pass that it was my job to clean the fish, always had been and always would be, I shall never know. No one ever taught me to do this. I was simply handed a sharp knife and told to scale, gut, and cut perfect filets off the bone, and I did. I was born knowing how to do this. And to this day I will not pass up an opportunity to do so.

Flounder, alas, I have never seen for sale where I live now. And whole fresh fish are very hard to come by of any species, even though Stockton, California, is a major port city.

The only exception is salmon. Happily, the butchers at my grocery, when they get a beautiful, whole wild king salmon, cut out wedges and bag the trimmings, which they sell for a few bucks. Sometimes the trimmings consist of the head and tail, sometimes other odds and ends. But there's usually a few pounds of salmon left on them, and there's nothing better than trimming it off carefully on a relaxed morning to make gravlax. You can, of course, buy whole pieces and just slice them thinly, too. Traditionally, you buy a whole side and cure it all and slice after, but this works just as well.

Place the thin slices of salmon on a board and generously sprinkle with salt and pepper on both sides. Then lay on sprigs of fresh baby dill. If you want to add other herbs, that's fine, and a splash of vodka is nice. I've even used pear brandy, which was wicked. Aquavit with caraway is ideal if you can find it.

Then just put the salmon in a sturdy plastic bag, place in the fridge, and put some heavy things on top. Every day turn it over, and after five days or a week, it's ready to use. Not exactly raw, but cured. If you want to, this would be the time to cold-smoke it, over fruit wood, very gently and for no more than an hour or so, as otherwise it can dry out or, worse, get cooked.

The most obvious venue for your gravlax is on a bagel with a "schmear" such as cream cheese. But it is just as good on rye toast or even serious crackers with chèvre. When you have a few pounds of gravlax in the fridge, you're supplied for a few weeks of noshing. And if you're tired of quick sandwiches, mix it into your omelet; sear it, and serve on rice; or even cook, cool, and add mayo for an extraordinary salmon salad with lettuce and other greens. It is among the most delicious and versatile ingredients you can have on hand.

CHICKPEA BAGEL WITH TARAMASALATA

In texture a chickpea bagel is somewhere between a drop biscuit and a crumbly cookie, rather than chewy like a wheat bagel. It pairs beautifully with Mediterranean flavors. Smoked trout with dukkah is very pleasant, as is tuna salad with a spot of harissa. But there is something magical about tarama—the salted roe of cod or other fish, mixed with olive oil and lemon juice and usually a little bread or potato as thickener. I have no idea why it is easily found in every grocery in Britain but difficult to find in the United States, unless there is a large Greek community nearby. Happily, the internet resolves such problems, and it is indeed mailed with ice packs.

1 C chickpea flour	2 tsp cream
1 tsp baking powder	1 tsp sesame seeds
¼ tsp salt	4 Tbs taramasalata
2 tsp buttermilk powder	A few baby spinach and chard leaves
1 egg	

Preheat your oven to 375°F. Mix the first six ingredients (chickpea flour, baking powder, salt, buttermilk powder, egg, and cream), setting aside a little of the egg in a small bowl for brushing. You should have a firm if sticky dough. Flatten it into a disk and poke a hole in the center. Place the dough on parchment paper, brush with the reserved egg, and sprinkle with sesame seeds. Bake for 20 minutes. Let cool thoroughly, and then slice horizontally. Spread a little taramasalata on each side, add some of the greens, finely shredded, and then add more taramasalata on top.

BIALYS WITH POT ROAST

The bialy is often called the lesser cousin of the bagel, but that's really not fair. The two have nothing to do with each other apart from a similar provenance in Poland and the fact that New York bagel bakers usually carried bialys too—but they rarely baked them themselves. A bialy is not boiled like a bagel, it's a much simpler dough and lends itself to home baking much more readily. It's just a round of basic yeasted dough, with a dimple in the middle, stuffed with onion and poppy. Nonetheless, a bialy can be sliced and treated exactly like a bagel or have the kind of attention lavished upon it as in this recipe. Make both parts the night before.

½ Tbs instant yeast	½ small onion
½ C water at 110°F	1 Tbs poppy seeds
¼ tsp unrefined sugar	1 tsp oil
1 ½ C bread flour	Pinch of salt
¼ tsp sea salt	

Pot Roast
2 lb chuck roast of beef (shoulder)
1 Tbs olive oil
1 tsp sea salt
2 small leeks
2 small carrots
1 stalk celery
½ bottle pinot noir
1 C rich beef stock
2 sprigs of thyme

Proof the yeast in the water and sugar, about 5 minutes until frothy. Mix in the flour and knead for 5 minutes until smooth and springy. Divide into four balls and place on a piece of parchment paper. Cover with a dishcloth and let rise for 1 hour. Chop the onion finely, and cook with the poppy seeds very lightly in the oil, with a pinch of salt. Let cool, and make an indentation in the center of each bialy and put a little of the onion mixture in the center. Be messy, getting some seeds on the bun, too. Heat the oven to 400°F and bake the bialys for 15 minutes. Let cool and keep them for the next day.

At the same time you make the bialys, start the beef. In a small, enameled cast-iron pot, sprinkle the beef with salt and brown it in the oil, turning it over so all sides are seared. Split the aromatic vegetables and add them to the pot, brown for a few minutes, then add all the other ingredients. Bring to gentle simmer and let cook on the lowest possible heat for 3 hours. Turn the beef over a few times while cooking. When finished cooking, let cool, then remove the beef and strain the liquid through a fine-mesh sieve. Discard the vegetables, pour the broth over the beef, and let sit overnight in the fridge. In the morning, remove any excess fat that has risen to the top (you can use the fat in another dish). Reheat a small amount of the pot roast and place it on a bialy that has been split and toasted. A little grating of fresh horseradish is ideal, or if you're feeling really opulent, mix horseradish into sour cream and place on top.

Bialys

Wraps

Almost all civilizations have some form of flat bread rolled around ingredients and held in the hand. Easy to assemble, eminently portable, it makes an ideal vehicle for carrying an array of foods and a perfect nosh, too. We will cover corn tortillas and dosas, injera and lefse, and all other relatives elsewhere; here we are devoted solely to wheat flour flat bread. This alone encompasses pita, naan and chapati, flour tortillas, and hundreds of other varieties. They are, of course, not interchangeable traditionally, but for noshing—and assuming you may not have access to excellent flat bread—I will include a simple recipe first that might stand in for most varieties. It is not the sort of thing anyone is likely to make first thing in the morning, but flatbreads hold up well for several days if you make a small batch of half a dozen in your free time. Under normal circumstances, I promise you, I use large, store-bought flour tortillas. They're okay. Store-bought pita I find execrable. If you can find it, lavash is excellent. It's an Armenian bread, rather like a huge round cracker. You moisten it with water, let it sit about an hour or more until softened, and then wrap it around the ingredients. But here's how to make fresh pita.

FRESH PITA

1 Tbs dry yeast
Small pinch of unrefined sugar
1 C water
3 C bread flour
½ tsp salt

Put the yeast in a large mixing bowl with the pinch of sugar, and pour hot tap water (about 110°F) over. You can judge the water temperature easily. Think of a cup of coffee, which is about 170–180°F—way too hot, and it will kill the yeast. Now think of hot water from your tap, which is about 120°F—still too hot. You want it somewhere between your body temperature and hot tap water. Or you can just use a kitchen thermometer. Wait about 5 minutes until the yeast froths up. No need to stir. Then slowly mix in the flour and lastly the salt. That's it. Wait a few minutes, then transfer the dough to a floured wooden board and knead for about 10 minutes. You'll probably need to add more flour, which is fine. Return the dough to the floured bowl and let rise for an hour, covered with a dry dishcloth.

Next, divide the dough into six equal balls and roll them aggressively between your well-floured hands. Place a large nonstick pan on the stovetop, and turn on two gas burners as high as they will go—the one under the pan, and another bare. Roll out your first pita into a flat round. Place it in the pan. Immediately start rolling out the next ball of dough. After 30 seconds turn the pita in the pan over. In the next 30 seconds finish rolling out the next raw pita. Move the cooked pita onto the open flame and the next raw pita into the hot pan. Keep your eye on the fire. A few seconds on each side over the open flame, and your pita may even puff up beautifully. (This is about 400 grams flour to 240 grams water, which is 60% hydration. A little more water will ensure it puffs up, but it makes the dough harder to work with.) If it doesn't puff up, no matter. Transfer it immediately to a plate and cover with another plate. This little steaming session is crucial.

If it takes a little time between rolling, cooking in the pan, and charring over flame, don't worry. There is no race to the finish. The more you do this, the more adept you'll become. Eventually you'll be able to rip through a batch of six in 15 minutes easily. If you don't have a gas stove, don't worry: the grill is just as good, maybe even better in terms of flavor, and a hot oven is also fine—crank it as hot as it will go and simply bake all the pitas at once on sheet pans.

When you're done with all the balls of dough, you'll have a lovely, warm stack of chewy pitas between the plates. To store, let cool thoroughly, put in a sealable plastic bag and store in the fridge. They warm up easily over the gas jet again. If you can resist scooping up hummus or baba ghanoush with them, here are the wraps.

TURKEY WRAP

1 flatbread, homemade or store-bought flour tortilla
2 Tbs chèvre
1 Tbs umeboshi plum paste (can be found in a Japanese grocery)
¼ C walnuts, crushed
1 tsp unrefined sugar
¼ tsp salt
⅛ tsp ground cinnamon
3 slices leftover turkey or roasted turkey cold cuts

Dressing
1 tsp apple cider vinegar
1 tsp maple syrup
1 Tbs walnut oil
Pinch of salt
Handful of baby spinach

Warm the flatbread over an open flame. Then spread with the chèvre and squirt on the umeboshi paste. This is a stand-in for cranberry sauce; it's more sour and salty, and sits in the wrap better. Spread it around evenly. Heat the crushed walnuts in a nonstick pan with the sugar and salt and cinnamon, stirring constantly and being careful not to let burn. Transfer to a plate to cool. Then sprinkle the nuts onto the flatbread. Add the slices of turkey. In a small bowl mix the vinegar, syrup, oil, and salt to form a dressing. Add the spinach, and mix with your hands. Then transfer to the flatbread. Roll up the bread tightly, cut on the diagonal, and serve at once.

TAMAGO WRAP

I've been making tamago wraps for many years with subtle variations, but I always return to this strange and remarkable combination of flavors. It is standard noshing fare for me.

1 round flatbread or flour tortilla
2 Tbs cream cheese
1 tsp wasabi or more to taste
1 jumbo egg or two smaller ones
2 Tbs dashi stock

1 tsp oil
⅓ C fresh cooked crab meat or imitation crab (surimi), shredded
Sprinkle of furikake

Heat the flatbread over the open flame of a gas burner on both sides. Let cool. Spread first with the cream cheese and then with the wasabi. Beat the egg with the dashi stock. You can use instant dashi or make the stock with katsuobushi flakes and kombu—or even shave a whole katsuobushi (a dried, smoked wedge of skipjack tuna). Take a pan the same size as your flatbread, heat the pan with the oil, and pour in the egg, tilting to cover the entire surface but not stirring. Drop the crab onto the surface. Cover the pan and cook gently until solid. Slide this onto your tortilla. Sprinkle with furikake and roll up. Cut into four even, sushi-shaped rolls, trimming off the uneven edges. Stack them facing upward on a plate, and eat while still warm.

LAVASH ARAM WRAP

If you can find the huge round lavash cracker bread, the "aram sandwich" is a great nosh you can prepare the night before and have waiting in the fridge for morning. Start by running tap water over the cracker until fairly soaked; cover with a damp towel or place in a large plastic bag until soft and pliable. Then layer in the ingredients, roll it up tightly, and wrap in plastic. Slice it into rounds. Each cracker will make enough for a few people, so you might want to just make half if it's just for you. Soft sandwich wraps are also available in stores, so if you like, you can skip the whole soaking phase.

Fill with crushed chickpeas, feta cheese, and bitter arugula leaves (dandelion is also great). Any kind of leftover vegetable is fine, but eggplant is excellent, as is any soft vegetable well cooked in olive oil and tomato, such as wide Romano string beans. Make the latter by cutting off the tips of the beans and stewing the beans slowly for an hour or longer in water, olive oil, and 4 or 5 grated roma tomatoes (discarding the skins), plenty of oregano, and salt. When they are soft and the water is almost all evaporated, they're done. They are fabulous cold, but even better in this wrap.

RICE WRAPPERS WITH CHICKEN LEGS

The confluence of chewy, noodle-like rice paper wrapper, crunchy vegetables, and a savory sauce is both refreshing and eye-opening, the perfect choice in hotter months when you don't want to cook. If you're lucky enough to have leftovers in the fridge, you are just a few seconds from a gorgeous and quick cold meal. Traditionally, Vietnamese rice paper rolls, or *gỏi cuốn*, are made with shrimp or pork, lettuce, rice noodles, and a dipping sauce like *nước chấm* (fish sauce, shallots, lime juice, and chilies), but I see no reason not to include whatever is on hand, as long as you maintain a good balance of savory, crunchy, and chewy.

I had leftover fried chicken legs in the fridge that day. They might have been the best I've ever made, marinated in buttermilk and a riot of herbs and spices (mustard powder, Old Bay, paprika, cumin, thyme, garlic powder, salt), dredged in Japanese flour, and fried in excellent rendered lard (not the flavorless hydrogenated stuff). Just one leg, shredded and divided between two wrappers, was plenty. I went a little berserk with the additions, but it all really was staring at me in the fridge.

2 large rice paper wrappers
1 leftover fried chicken leg, shredded
Handful finely shredded romaine lettuce
5 or 6 large basil leaves, rolled and cut as a chiffonade
Handful of bean sprouts
1 Tbs dry-roasted, salted peanuts, crushed
2 Tbs chili garlic crunch condiment
A few squirts of ranch dressing
Loosely torn cilantro to garnish

Run the wrappers under hot water for about 10 seconds and lay them flat on the counter. Place a few pieces of chicken, the vegetables, and nuts inside and fold over the bottom edge. Then fold over the two sides and roll up into a neat little package. Place the rolls on a plate and spread over them the chili sauce, the dressing, and cilantro. Knife and fork required if constructed as I did here.

Rice Wrappers with Chicken Legs

Purple Potato Lefse Wrap

PURPLE POTATO LEFSE WRAP

In Norway there is a perfectly delightful, thin and soft flatbread called lefse, made with potatoes. It somewhat resembles gnocchi in flavor. A friend once gave me a long, flat stick painted red with white flowers, used for turning the lefse over. It's so pretty that I've never used it. A pair of tongs or even your fingers work fine if you're brave. This recipe is an adaptation using purple potatoes, plus a little butterfly pea flower to ramp up the color. The taste is nothing alarming, though. You can put in any filling; hot dogs are common in Scandinavia, but I really like raw salmon and a little added crunch with rutabaga.

4 small, thin slices raw salmon
Salt and pepper
2 small purple potatoes
An equal amount of bread
　　flour, about ½–⅓ C
2 tsp Greek yogurt

½ tsp butterfly pea flower powder
　　(*Ternatea clitoria*; you
　　can purchase it online)
2 Tbs cream cheese
2 Tbs capers
½ C raw rutabaga, grated

Slice a piece of salmon into thin pieces, and salt and pepper generously. This can be done well in advance, even up to a few days. Keep in the fridge.

Put your potatoes in the microwave for 3 minutes. Cut in half and let cool slightly, then scoop out the insides into a bowl. Add a roughly equal amount of bread flour, and the yogurt and pea flower, which is a lurid purple. You may need a little more yogurt to keep the dough from cracking. Work it all together with your hands until it's a smooth dough. Lay a large sheet of plastic wrap on your cutting board and form the dough into a disk. Pinch the edges closed if they begin to crack a little. Cover that with another sheet of plastic and then roll out into a large flat bread. Heat a large, nonstick frying pan on the stove, and then carefully remove the top piece of plastic and turn your lefse over and into the pan. Quickly remove the other piece of plastic. Let cook on one side about 1 minute, shaking to make sure it doesn't stick. Then use tongs to turn it over, or just turn it onto the palm of your hand and flip it over. Cook another few minutes, until you see the dough puff up here and there, and brown spots emerge. Place between two large plates and let cool.

Spread one side with the cream cheese. If you can find the soft, spreadable kind, all the better. Peel and grate a small wedge of rutabaga and lightly salt it. Add on top of the cream cheese and sprinkle on some capers. Add the salmon. Roll the lefse tightly, cut on a diagonal and serve.

TEMAKI WITH COUSCOUS, QUINOA, OR FONIO WRAP

Sushi is among my favorite foods, and I thought it would be interesting to switch out the rice for other grains. I've done this before with success, filling grape leaves with other grains, and stuffing peppers as well. It becomes tricky using nori wrappers because the grains squish out when you try to slice the roll. The temaki hand roll, in a cone, works much better—and in the case of couscous, this really does only take a few minutes to assemble. You could also use quinoa, amaranth, or my new favorite, fonio, which is a tiny grain from West Africa that is simple to cook. Follow the package directions for cooking each grain type.

½ C water	1 Tbs soy
1 tsp butter	¼ tsp freshly grated ginger
Pinch of salt	1 Tbs dry sake
½ C couscous	Furikake flakes
2 nori sheets	1 dab mayonnaise
Raw salmon without	1 dab katsu sauce
skin—about 2 oz	

Heat the water and add the butter and salt. When it comes to a boil, remove from the heat and add the couscous. Cover and let sit for 5 minutes.

While the couscous is resting, cut the salmon into small pieces and marinate in the soy, ginger, and sake for 5 minutes. Then mix with the couscous, fluffing it up with a fork.

Roll the sheets of nori into a narrow cone and place in a champagne flute. Fill each with the couscous mixture. It should reach the top, and you might have a little left over. If you like, cut off the top of the seaweed with pinking shears to give a decorative edge. Top with the furikake, mayo, and sauce.

Temaki with Couscous, Quinoa, or Fonio Wrap

XAWAASH CHICKEN, LENTILS, AND RAITA ON ROTI WRAP

This is obviously something you need to start the day before. Cook the whole thing for dinner, making extra for leftovers, or prepare a small batch just so you have a magnificent nosh. In either case, this recipe jumbles various flavors from around the coasts of the Indian Ocean. The xawaash is a spice mix that I first tasted in Alaska, where I met a group of Somali women at a farming cooperative and bought a jar. You can buy it online already mixed, or make it yourself. Mix cumin, coriander, pepper, cardamom, cloves, and cinnamon in roughly equal proportion. You can also add turmeric and ginger, but then it seems to me more like a curry powder, which is also very good. Seriously, the mix is up to you.

> 2 Tbs butter
> 1 medium yellow onion
> 1 tsp salt
> 1 small red bell pepper, chopped
> 1 small jalapeño pepper, chopped
> 1 Tbs xawaash spice
> 2 boneless, skinless chicken thighs
> 4 Roma tomatoes
> 1 Tbs peanut butter
> 1 C water

Melt the butter in a small pot. Chop the onion finely and add with ½ tsp salt. Cook gently until browned. Add the chopped peppers, then the spice. Mix thoroughly. Sprinkle the chicken with remaining salt. Then nestle it down into the onion mixture and cook until browned lightly on both sides. Slice the tomatoes in half, and place the cut side down on a large-holed grater, grating all the tomato (except the skins) directly into the pot. Add the peanut butter and water, and then simmer gently for an hour. Let cool and place in the fridge overnight to let the flavors meld.

While this is happening, simmer a cup of lentils in a pot, covered with water with a teaspoon of salt, until tender. Place that in a container in the fridge, too.

The next day, get a lump of flatbread dough about the size of your fist. (See the recipe for fresh pita.) Roll it into a round on a floured board and cook on a hot (ungreased) nonstick pan for 45 seconds. Turn it over and cook for another 30 seconds. Then place it directly over an open flame until it puffs up, turning over often with tongs so it doesn't burn. Place on a plate and spread on a teaspoon of butter. This is the roti. Warm up the chicken and the lentils in the microwave for a couple of minutes each. Spread them on the dough. Then mix ¼ peeled and chopped cucumber with a¼ cup of yogurt and a pinch of salt (this is your raita). Add that, too. Roll up the flat bread, slice diagonally, and serve.

Xawaash Chicken, Lentils, and Raita on Roti Wrap

LAMBS IN A BLANKET

At first glance this sounds like something no one could ever do at home, but let me assure you that it's simple, and though it takes a little time and patience, surprisingly no machinery whatsoever is involved. If you are making sausages in any volume, then I suppose machines are a good idea. This recipe makes four, which you can eat through the week. The advantage to making your own is that you can put in exactly the kind of flavorings you like. Those I used here may sound a little outlandish, but they are exactly the sort of flavor combination Italian cookbook authors like Messisbugo or Scappi would have preferred in the sixteenth century. As for the casings, you can buy them online. A small bag of salted casings is inexpensive and will last more than a year. In the end, these are sort of like sausage rolls, which are a glorious thing, but the dough isn't puff pastry, which I find tastes greasy and goes soggy unless it's right out of the oven.

Sausages
About 3 feet of hog casings, 35 mm in diameter (1 ¼–1 ½ inches)
1 lb ground lamb
1 ½ tsp fine sea salt
¼ tsp Insta Cure #2
1 Tbs grated rind of 1 organic orange without the white pith
10 ground cloves

Dough
1 Tbs dry yeast
1 C water at 110°F
½ tsp unrefined sugar
3 C bread flour
1 tsp salt
1 egg
½ tsp za'atar

Sauce
1 Tbs tahini paste
¼ C fresh orange juice
½ tsp rice wine vinegar
¼ tsp sugar
¼ tsp salt

Soak the casings in water, changing the water frequently and rinsing the insides, about half an hour. Meanwhile, mix the other ingredients well. Cut the casings into four equal lengths. Holding one end open, put pinches of the meat inside and squeeze down with your fingers. You can also use a wide-mouth funnel, but I find this method quicker. Don't squeeze too hard or the casings will split. Fill the other side, and then tie off each end with a string. Repeat with the rest of the casings, and you'll have four 6 inch sausages. Tie off the ends with string, and cut off the excess casings. Put in a plastic bag and let cure in the fridge for at least a day, or up to several days.

Proof the yeast with the water and sugar for about 10 minutes until frothy. Mix in the flour and salt, and knead for about 5 minutes. Place in a floured bowl and let rise 1 hour. Then remove from the bowl and divide into four balls. Roll these out into long even coils with your hands. Twist them, and then wrap each coil of dough around a sausage, encasing all but the ends, which should stick out just a little. Brush each one with beaten egg and sprinkle with za'atar or dried thyme. Let these rise at room temperature about an hour. Then preheat an oven to 350°F and bake them for 45 minutes.

Serve with the tahini sauce. Mustard is really good, too. Eat one now, and wrap the others in tinfoil to eat later in the week or freeze them. To defrost, just warm up in a toaster oven.

Lambs in a Blanket

CHEUNG FUN MANICOTTI WITH CRAB AND GREEN MANGO

Cheung Fun is a thick chewy rice wrapper from Asia that functions much the same way as manicotti in Italy. I had to test this recipe at least nine times. I had a good idea of how it should be made and then proceeded to tweak every individual step, sometimes looking to see how other people did it, and then falling short every single time. I tried half a dozen different types of steamers, too. Finally I asked a Chinese friend, who gave me a very simple set of ingredients and proportions—to be cooked in the microwave no less—and it worked wonderfully. I just cut that basic recipe down to a single serving. Nonetheless, I couldn't help but mess with it. Traditionally this would be served with soy sauce or something similar, but the tomato sauce was there calling to me, and the combination of crab and tomato is so alluring, I couldn't resist.

Note: I don't know why in the United States rice starch is called rice flour. Or why in Britain cornstarch is called corn flour. Starch feels dry and powdery between the fingers, like talc, unlike whole flour, which is soft. Here you want starch, whatever they call it.

¼ C rice starch (usually labeled "flour")
1 ½ tsp cornstarch
½ tsp wheat starch
6 Tbs cool water
1 ½ tsp canola oil, plus more for greasing the plastic

1 ½ C cooked blue swimmer crab or other type
1 tsp mayonnaise
1 tiny green sour mango
3 Tbs tomato sauce
3 sprigs parsley, chopped

Mix the starches, water, and oil in a bowl. Get an 8″ × 8″ glass Pyrex or ceramic casserole with a flat bottom. Cut a piece of thick plastic, such as from a zip-top freezer bag, and use it to cover the bottom, leaving the edges hanging over. Grease it lightly with oil. This step is essential for getting the noodle out. Pour in the batter and microwave on high heat for 1 minute and 20 seconds. (Depending on your microwave, you may need a few seconds more or less.) Let the noodle cool for a minute, and then lift the plastic out with the noodle attached.

Next, mix the crabmeat with a little mayo to moisten, and place it in the noodle, lined up on one end. Peel and slice the mango and add that. Using the plastic, tightly roll the filling up in the noodle until it forms a cylinder and is separated from the plastic. Transfer to a plate, spread on the sauce, and top with the parsley. You may want to reheat everything together for 30 seconds or so in the microwave before adding parsley and serving.

Cheung Fun Manicotti with Crab and Green Mango

BBQ CHICKEN WRAP

This is a great way to recycle leftover chicken. You can really use any part, but I had wings, made very simply by seasoning with salt, pepper, oregano, cayenne, and cumin, then grilling, then tossing in a pan with a knob of butter and barbecue sauce until sticky. Just take the meat off the bones, shred finely, and reheat in the microwave for about 20 seconds.

Wrap
2 large rice paper wrappers
6 BBQ chicken wings
1 jalapeño
1 small carrot

Sauce
1 lime
2 Tbs fish sauce
1 scallion
1 tsp palm sugar
1 tsp peanut butter

Run a wrapper under hot water for about 5 seconds, and lay it flat on your work surface. Place a line of half the chicken shreds at one end, then half the carrot and chili. Fold over the ends and roll up the contents tightly. Very lightly anoint with oil so they don't stick to the plate. Repeat with the second wrap.

For the sauce, squeeze your lime, and add the other ingredients, stirring until smooth. Serve in a little bowl for dipping your wraps into.

BBQ Chicken Wrap

Pizzas

Everyone knows that sandwiches are the perfect nosh, but pizza actually ascends higher as the perfect food itself. There's a lot of bad pizza out there, but the technique is less complicated than people pretend. To make a great pizza at home is perfectly possible, even without a wood-burning stove at 900°F, 00 flour imported from Italy, along with the buffalo mozzarella and San Marzano tomatoes crushed by hand. What I love most about pizza is that, however it is made, it has no pretension. It is what it is, whether laced with caviar or ham and pineapple or desecrated in a way that would make the Associazione Verace Pizza Napoletana writhe in torment.

PIZZA DOUGH AND TIPS FOR GREAT PIZZA

If you have the time to start a dough the day before and put it in the fridge, you'll find that with time the glutens develop on their own, the flavor becomes more complex, and it's even easier to work with. Sometimes, when I wake up early, I start a dough even without this prolonged fermentation. An hour is plenty of time. When making pizza for dinner, I always begin making the dough around 5:00 p.m. But having some dough in the fridge means that anytime you like, you can pinch off a bit, make a pizza any size, and nosh.

Start by proofing 1 tablespoon of yeast with a pinch of sugar in 110°F water. The yeast will bubble up and get frothy. Add 3 cups of flour and 1 teaspoon of salt. Then put the dough on a floured board and knead about 5 minutes. Put it in a floured bowl (or an oiled bowl works fine, too) and let it rise about an hour. Or if you're using it the next day, just put it in a large plastic bag, which has been lightly oiled, and toss in the fridge. This is enough to make two thick or three thin pizzas. So if you're making a noshing pizza, I'd say use about one-quarter of the dough or less, a good handful.

The ideal way to deal with the dough is to roll it out on a piece of parchment paper, which will make transferring it to the oven much easier. Preheat your oven to 500°F or as hot as it will get. If you have a pizza stone, all the better—put it in the oven while preheating. Then tear mozzarella into small nubbins with your hand and place directly on the pizza first. I know this is not the way it's usually done, but it will prevent the toppings from sliding off. Then add your vegetables, meats, or whatever you like, and last of all drizzle on the sauce. I like a very simple passata from a bottle—just enough for flavoring. Put the pizza with the paper on a baker's peel and slide onto the stone. If you don't have this equipment, just cook it on a baking sheet. I also throw a few ice cubes in the bottom of the oven to create steam, which gives a good rise in the crust. It will take about 10 minutes, but watch carefully. It's not likely to burn, but you want the top nicely gooey and the crust lightly browned and crisp.

Now, if starting up the oven for a nosh doesn't appeal to you, place the dough directly into a very hot, dry nonstick pan. Turn it over a few times until nicely colored on both sides, lower the heat way down. Add the toppings just as before and leave on the stove until they melt. Then just place the pizza under the broiler for a minute or so to cook the top through. The effect isn't quite the same as when done in the oven, but it's very good nonetheless. As they say, pizza is like sex. Even when it's bad, it's still pretty good.

SANDWICH PIZZA

I'm sure you're thinking that you've seen this before: two slices of leftover pizza with some ingredients inside and stuffed together face to face with the lower crusts creating two outer sides. That's a pizza sandwich. This is quite different and involves a little dexterity with a serrated bread knife. First, you need a fairly thick slice of pizza, left over from the night before. Place it on a cutting board and insert the tip of the serrated knife into the edge of the outer crust. With a light sawing motion, divide the outer crust horizontally, slowly turning the slice of pizza as you cut. Proceed to divide the rest of the crust in similar fashion. What you should now have is one wedge of bare lower crust and one wedge of the upper crust with tomato and cheese, etc. Do you see why this would be impossible with a thin pie?

Now slather the two bare sides with mayonnaise, and sprinkle with some paprika, herbs, or other flavorful dry condiment. Then slice up some leftover fried chicken and place it inside the pizza, and put back the top. Add a little more homemade tomato sauce or jarred passata and mozzarella cheese on top of the pizza wedge and place in a toaster oven to heat through.

Consider the possibilities here. Any kind of leftover can go inside: slices of fried eggplant or zucchini, steak or pork chop, sautéed mushrooms, even cooked beans work well, if you don't mind getting a little messy. It is an ideal way to make something exciting out of scraps in your fridge in just a few quick minutes. And it is almost always better than the pizza from the night before.

FLATBREAD PIZZA

I make this at least once a week as a nosh or even for breakfast. Once you have the technique down, you will be able to do it in your sleep. I will explain the technique and leave the exact ingredients to you, because that is the entire point. Play with this a little every time you make it. Add or remove ingredients. Eventually you will discover the combinations that you love best.

To start, take an ordinary flour tortilla. I use those intended for burritos, which fit comfortably in my nonstick frying pan. Using a pair of tongs, warm the tortilla directly over an open flame, turning frequently until both sides are slightly charred. If you don't have gas burners, use the broiler, or even a blowtorch held at a distance. The tortilla will puff up, so be ready for a little drama. Then place it in the frying pan over low heat. With your fingers, break up about ¼ cup of low-moisture whole-milk mozzarella into small nubbins and place on the bread. You don't want it shredded, just little lumps with bare, exposed bread showing through. Fresh mozzarella, as lovely as it is, will not work here. Then mix a small can of tuna, drained, with mayonnaise. Pinch little bits of this and place it between the nubbins of cheese. Then drain some capers and scatter them around evenly. Chopped olives work just as well. Then crumble a little dried rosemary on top, and finally, slice some tiny cherry tomatoes and arrange those on top. As you can see, there is no sauce and it is constructed backward, so the base will be crisp.

As you are adding the ingredients, keep checking the bottom and rotating the pizza to make sure it isn't burning. You want it crunchy but not blackened. When it is crisp, place the whole pan under the broiler for just a few seconds until the cheese bubbles and the edges begin to brown. Cut it into six wedges and enjoy. The whole process should take no more than 10 minutes.

Now let your imagination kick in. Any leftover vegetable is great here. I often have a little broccoli rabe or other sautéed greens. A creamy feta cheese substitutes in perfectly. So does a good Gruyère, but then I'd add shiitake mushrooms, sliced and sautéed in butter. Of course, any traditional pizza topping, such as pepperoni, sausage, peppers, and onions, is fantastic here, too.

Let me also suggest that if you have the forethought to have some fresh pizza dough in the fridge, it can also be used for a quick little pizza. Just roll out a handful of dough. Cook it briefly in the heated pan first, then put it over an open flame to puff up, then back into the pan. Then proceed as described above.

SALAD PIZZA

This is technically more of an Indian naan dough rather than pizza dough because it's unrisen. Traditionally the naan is cooked in a tandoor oven, slapped on the side clay wall of the cylindrical oven that has a fire burning at the bottom, and comes out light and flaky. At home, a nonstick pan works fine, and as you're only making one, this is a remarkably quick recipe.

½ C bread flour
½ tsp salt
¼ C (approx.) unflavored
    Greek yogurt

½ C arugula
¼ C cotija or feta cheese
2 cherry tomatoes, sliced
1 hard-boiled quail egg, sliced

For the dough, mix together the bread flour, salt, and Greek yogurt. You will have to feel the dough to judge how much yogurt to add. It should be firm and not too sticky, so add more yogurt if it's too hard and dry, or more flour if it's too wet. This will depend entirely on your flour, the yogurt, the weather, and the whim of the gods. Knead for about 5 minutes. Roll out into a round flatbread on a floured board. Heat your pan on high. Place the bread directly in it and cook about 45 seconds. Turn over and cook another 30 seconds. Add the other ingredients, and place under the broiler for a few minutes until everything is melted and bubbly—but be sure to remove it before the edges burn. Cut into wedges and eat.

Salad Pizza

TORTA DE ACEITE

If you've never had one of these light and crunchy disks popular in Spain, it's not only very easy to make, but also serves as a base for practically anything. Here I've taken it one step further and turned it into a kind of pizza. Just get a glass of very dry sherry and listen to the most doleful Flamenco singer you can find.

1 tsp yeast	⅛ tsp salt
¼ C water at 110°F	1 tsp unrefined sugar
3 Tbs olive oil	1 tsp grated parmesan cheese
1 C flour	4 anchovies
1 tsp fennel	6 green olives

In a mixing bowl, combine the yeast and the water and let the mixture get frothy. Add the olive oil, flour, fennel, and salt. Knead well for a few minutes and then divide into four small balls. You won't need to flour your board, just roll these out into rounds about the size of your hand and place them on a parchment paper–lined cookie sheet. Let rise uncovered for 1 hour. The "rise" will be practically imperceptible, but it's necessary.

Take two of the rounds and sprinkle sugar on them; sprinkle parmesan, chopped olives, and anchovies on the other two. Bake in a 400°F oven for 8 minutes. The sugar should just have begun to melt on the sweet ones. Let them cool to crisp up. Eat the two savory ones for breakfast, and save the other two for your late afternoon collation.

Torta de Aceite

LACHHA PARATHA AND BUSS UP SHUT

These are two closely related dishes. The first comes from Punjab, and is a richly layered, buttery flatbread. The other is a variation from Trinidad (where Indians were sent under British rule), in which the ragged bread is busted up like an old shirt. There are dozens of different variations of the dish, often stuffed with cauliflower or other vegetables. I find that they also make very good bases for something like a pizza. Most important, they can actually be made very quickly, in about 15 minutes, without resting the dough at any point.

½ C bread flour
¼ C water
¼ tsp salt
¼ tsp oil
2 Tbs salted butter

Mix together the bread flour, water, salt, and oil, and knead vigorously for a couple of minutes. With a tapered pin, roll out the dough into the thinnest round shape you can. You shouldn't need any extra flour for the board at this point. Spread on the butter with a butter knife. You want it soft but still cold. Roll the entire round into a long thin cigar. Then coil the whole thing into a spiral, creating a tight circle. Now flour the board and roll out the dough once again into a large flat circle. If little bits of butter pop through, don't worry, just flour it a little more.

Heat up a large, nonstick skillet on high; don't add oil. Place the paratha in the skillet, and turn over every few minutes until charred in bits on both sides. The next and last step is essential: place the flatbread between two plates, one facing up, the other down, so the bread steams inside with its own moisture. This prevents it from drying out and creates a chewy/crispy texture.

At this point, you can put the paratha back in the hot pan, and add cheese, vegetables, and whatever toppings you like to make a kind of pizza. Cut into wedges and eat.

The Buss Up Shut is a similar technique but with a few crucial differences. To the same recipe given above, add ½ teaspoon milk powder or buttermilk powder. Instead of spiraling, you will roll up the dough a little differently. After you've buttered the rolled-out dough, imagine the circle to be the face of a clock. Cut a notch from the center to top at 12 o'clock. Start rolling up the dough from the right side, clockwise, exactly as the second hand sweeps, until you reach 3 o'clock, then 6, then 9, then 12. You'll have a long cone. Tuck in the edges of the wide end and then the tapered end and stand it up straight like a tall cone. Squash it into a flat circle. All the butter should still be encased.

Roll that disk out again, flouring the board well, and scraping any stray bits of butter off your board and pin. Then heat a large nonstick pan, and this time butter it a little. Place the flat bread in the pan, and cook on both sides. Also, sprinkle on a little water now and then, on both sides. I suppose this lets it cook longer without burning. Keep going until charred here and there. And now the exciting part: bust it up with two forks until you have a messy tangle of flaky bits. It is magnificent.

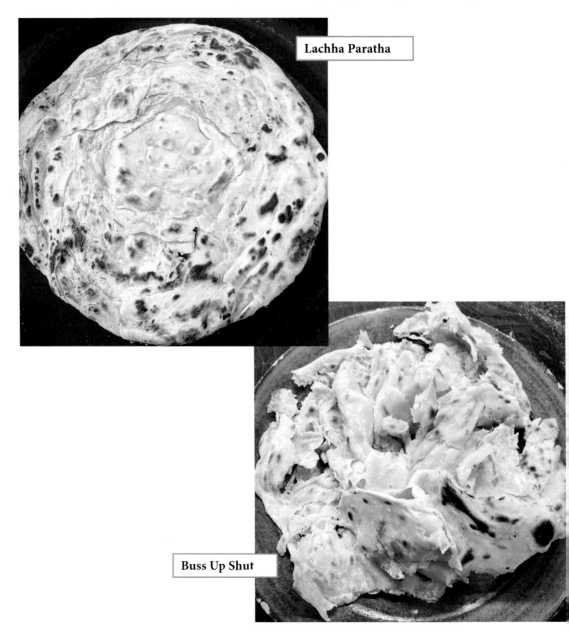

Lachha Paratha

Buss Up Shut

LAHMACUN WITH DUCK AND PINEAPPLE

A distant cousin to the pizza, this flatbread covered in spicy chopped meat hails from Armenia and Turkey. Traditionally it's made with ground lamb or beef seasoned with spices and tomato, but no cheese. It's also small enough to roll up and eat on the go, so very different from pizza. Here, I put my leftovers to good use, and the combination of the earthy spices and heat with cooked pineapple is truly delightful, if unusual.

Dough
1 tsp yeast
⅓ C hot water
Pinch sugar
2 Tbs semolina flour
7 Tbs bread flour
½ tsp olive oil
⅛ tsp salt

Topping
1 small cooked duck leg and thigh
1 6-inch wedge fresh pineapple, trimmed and cored
3 Tbs tomato puree (passata)
Pinch each of ground allspice, cinnamon, urfa biber, cumin, and salt
1 green onion
Few sprigs cilantro
¼ lemon wedge

Mix the yeast, water, and sugar and let it all get frothy. Add the flours, oil, and salt, and knead for about 5 minutes. Ideally, you should do this the night before and keep it in the fridge. If not, let it rise for about 1 hour—but I often just start it in the morning, and by the time the oven is heated and the other ingredients prepared, about 20 minutes, I just proceed with the recipe.

While the dough is rising, chop the duck very finely, cut the pineapple into small nubbins, and cook both together with the tomato and spices. Add a little water if it gets dry, and taste for seasoning. You may want a little more salt or heat. Let the mixture cool about 5 minutes.

Preheat the oven to 500°F.

Roll the dough out into a circle about 10–12 inches in diameter. Spread the duck mixture on top, leaving a little bare edge. Transfer it to a floured peel and slide it into the oven. It should only take about 4–5 minutes. Remove it before the edges get brown; you want this soft and chewy rather than crisp.

When you've removed it from the oven, add the onion and cilantro, and squeeze on the lemon juice. You can eat it cut into wedges like a pizza, but I think it's good on a plate, torn with your fingers. It's also really good with some dressed salad right on top and rolled up.

Lahmacun with Duck and Pineapple

KHACHAPURI WITH SNAILS AND TRUFFLES

Once again, this is neither pizza nor a traditional khachapuri as would be made in Georgia (the country rather than the American state). The bosky aroma of this dish will have me making it more often. If you can't find a truffle, mushrooms are, of course, a fine substitute.

Dough	Filling
1 tsp yeast	1 leaf swiss chard
¼ C hot water	2 Tbs salted butter
⅛ tsp unrefined sugar	1 small clove garlic
¾ C flour	6 snails (canned)
Pinch of salt	2 oz toma cheese
	1 summer truffle
	⅛ tsp salt

The night before you want to eat this, mix the yeast and the hot water with the sugar and let sit until frothy. Add the flour and salt and knead about 10 minutes. Put into a lightly floured plastic bag in the fridge. The next day, take it out and preheat your oven to 500°F.

Shred the leaf of chard, discarding the tough stem. Cook in the butter for 1 minute, add the garlic, finely chopped, and then the snails. I used canned, but if you can find fresh, they are fabulous. Just remember that they need long purging while alive and then long boiling to remove the ooze. Cook everything together over low heat for just a few minutes.

Shape the dough into a boat with a good inch or more height in the sides. Break the cheese into small bits and place half inside. Slice the truffle and add that. Then add the snails and cover with the last bits of cheese. Slide onto a sheet of parchment paper and bake at 500°F for 10 minutes, when the crust will be nicely browned and the cheese bubbling. Eat with your fingers. You can add an egg on top too, but I didn't think the dish needed it.

Khachapuri with Snails and Truffles

PINSA ROMANA

Regardless of how many times you say this, people will ask whether this is *pizza*. It's a cousin, with apparently ancient roots. The version you are likely to find in Rome today is made from a combination of wheat, rice, soy, and chickpea flours that can even be bought as a prepared mix. It's a very wet dough and fermented much longer than usual, but the signature differences are the oval shape and light fluffy texture.

Dough
½ Tbs yeast
1 C hot (100°F) water
½ tsp unrefined sugar
1 C bread flour
1 ¼ C all-purpose (or Italian "00") flour
½ C rice starch
½ tsp salt

Toppings
6 oz mozzarella
4 stalks asparagus
1 tsp olive oil
6 thin slices hard boar salami
¼ C tomato passata

Mix the yeast, water, and sugar, and let it all get frothy. Add the other dry ingredients and mix well. Knead for about 5 minutes. Place in an oiled bowl and let rise about 2–3 hours (or place in the refrigerator overnight). The next day preheat your oven to 500°F, shred the cheese, peel the base of the asparagus, and chop the stalks. Cook lightly in olive oil. Chop the salami into thin shreds. Take half your dough, stretch it into an oval, and place on a baking sheet lined with parchment paper. Lay on the cheese and other toppings, and then add dollops of passata at the end. Bake for about 10 minutes. If you want to bake all the dough, make a second pinsa. You can add on anything you like, such as kale with pesto.

Pinsa Romana

Tacos, Tortillas, and Corn Cakes

LEFTOVER DUCK LEG TACOS

Any leftover meat works in this context, but somehow duck leg seems just right, especially the Muscovy ducks that they raise in my neck of the woods, descended from a species native to Mexico. They're big, black and white birds with an alarming patch of squiggly red wattle around the eyes. One of the main processing plants for these ducks is in downtown Stockton, California, where I live. I once brought a class for a visit, mostly young women, who were astounded by how calm and pleasant the whole operation turned out to be. For many years, the confit legs were available very cheap in my local grocery store, and then every year, for about a decade, the price went up a dollar or so for a pair, so now they're no longer so economical. If you can't find or make confit legs, regular duck legs are great instead. I grill them or marinate in soy and ginger and pan-fry. Just save a leg and thigh for a nosh the next day.

> 1 duck leg and thigh, confit or cooked otherwise
> 2 small, fresh white corn tortillas
> 2 sticks string cheese or roughly the equivalent Oaxaca melting cheese
> 5 or 6 walnuts, crushed
> 2 Tbs crunchy garlic chili condiment

Shred the cold duck and discard the skin and bones. Place the tortillas directly over an open gas flame, turning frequently until lightly charred on both sides. You can also grill them briefly or place close under the broiler. Then place each tortilla in a separate small pan over low heat. Shred the cheese and place it on the hot tortilla. Add the duck and walnuts. Leave on the heat until the bottom is crispy. Then place each pan under the broiler until it is hot and the cheese is bubbling. Spoon the chili over the taco and serve. To eat, fold each in half and hover above when biting into it, so you don't get sauce on your shirt.

Leftover Duck Leg Tacos

FLAUTA

Take a corn tortilla and warm it briefly, directly over an open flame. Then put a slice of mortadella on it and a stick of string cheese. Wrap it up and stick a toothpick through it to keep it rolled. Put it in a dry pan on low to heat through. Meanwhile, put a spoonful of yogurt in a small bowl, add some chopped cilantro, a squirt of lime, and a few drops of green hot sauce. Then add a few drops of oil to the pan to brown the tortilla. Serve. Dip the flauta in the sauce. Done.

BRUNOST TORTILLA WITH APPLES

This combination of flavors sounds outlandish and even absurd. But I promise you, upon tasting it, you will think of caramel corn, a caramel apple, cheese and apples, or some combination thereof. This cheese tastes like a combination of caramel and cheese and is actually made from whey, which is a by-product of cheesemaking. It's not too sweet, either, especially if you use very tart apples.

Brown a corn tortilla in a pan. Add shredded Norwegian brunost or gjetost on top and then slices of apple. Heat through and then sprinkle with cinnamon.

Brunost Tortilla with Apples

CHILAQSHUKA

Chilaquiles and shakshuka seem to be long-lost cousins. Why not bring them together again, and call the combination "chilaqshuka"? Usually both are made of sautéed chopped tomatoes and other vegetables with an egg cracked and cooked in the sauce, the former with tortillas, the latter best scooped up with flatbread. I have used tortilla chips, but then felt like I was eating nachos—great but ordinary. The chips also get a bit soggy when cooked together, so here I've put them around the other ingredients. I have used pita chips, too, and that worked well. This is a twist on both that would work either with leftover corn tortillas or stale pita. I also used tomatillos just because it sounded good.

> 3 small, stale corn tortillas or 2 small pitas
> 3 Tbs olive oil
> 6 or 7 tomatillos, chopped
> 2 green onions, sliced
> 1 serrano chili
> A few slices leftover skirt steak
> ¼ C leftover beans
> 1 egg
> 2 Tbs white cheddar, shredded
> 2 Tbs cilantro, chopped

Cut the tortillas into thin strips and fry gently in the olive oil until crisp. Transfer to a paper towel and season with salt. Add the tomatillos to the pan and fry in the same oil. Add the onion and chili, and cook down until it becomes a chunky sauce. Chop the steak and reheat it in another pan, and warm up the beans. Then break an egg into the center of the simmering tomatillos. Let cook through.

Arrange the tortilla strips in a circle on a plate and carefully scoop the egg into the center. Then surround with the rest of the sauce. Add the meat and beans all around too. Top with the cheese, cilantro, and some of the onions. If you like, proceed with the recipe as written, but use strips of pita bread instead of tortilla strips, and use feta instead of cheddar, lamb instead of beef, chickpeas and fresh parsley instead of cilantro. Or mix the ingredients up; any combination will be great.

Chilaqshuka

SAUSAGE GRAVY WITH CHEEZ WHIZ ON FRITOS

Sometimes I find myself chasing after the most rarefied, obscure ingredients. So once in a while it's important to get your bearings with something like this. Is this what they call Flavortown, Guy? Yes, this is also a perfect nosh for stoners.

1 C lightly salted Fritos
2 oz loose breakfast sausage
Pinch each of oregano, garlic
    powder, smoked paprika
1 Tbs flour

½ C milk
1 Tbs Cheez Whiz
2 jalapeño-stuffed olives
3 dashes of chipotle Tabasco sauce

Place the Fritos on a small plate. Fry the sausage until brown, breaking up with a spatula. Add the spices and flour, and stir over medium heat for 2 minutes. Stir in the milk, then the Cheez Whiz. Pour over the Fritos, and garnish with the olives, sliced. Season with Tabasco. Serve at once. You could also serve this right in the bag of chips, as is done with a "Frito pie."

Sausage Gravy with Cheez Whiz on Fritos

AREPAS

If you can find P.A.N. cornmeal, it is just about the easiest thing to make into flat cakes, which are cooked in a pan, split open, and filled. The corn is actually pre-cooked but not nixtamalized, so it's very different from regular cornmeal and masa harina. Take an amount of cornmeal, maybe a cup for one person, and add about an equal measure of water and a pinch of salt. That's it. Form into flat disks and cook in a pan, with or without oil, for about 5 minutes per side on medium-low heat. After splitting, you can also fry them, open side down, to make the inside crunchy. Leftovers or cold cuts are great in an arepa, but I had on hand a roasted yellow beet, simply cooked in an oven the night before. I peeled and sliced it, seasoned it with salt and oil and vinegar, and put it in the arepa with some pea sprouts. The combination was lovely.

Arepas

TLAYUDAS

Think of these as really big, thin, crispy tortillas, served either flat or folded up, as a street food, as is done in Oaxaca. They are traditionally cooked on a big clay comal over an open fire and filled with beans, lard, shredded meat, and cabbage. Here I used cheese, chicken, and cabbage, all shredded. You can use whatever you have. It's the technique, adapted for home cooking here, that I found so surprisingly satisfying.

½ C masa harina
Water
½ C cooked chicken, shredded
2 oz cheese, shredded
¼ C shredded cabbage

Start with the masa harina flour. Mix it with water, adding a little at a time, and knead until you have a smooth dough, not crumbly and not too sticky. Some brands, such as Masienda, will instruct you to let the dough rest for an hour. Next, lightly oil a 12 inch nonstick frying pan. Press the dough into the pan with your fingers, making a thin, even cake covering most of the surface. You'll have to fiddle with the edges to prevent them from cracking, but that's fairly easy to do. Then put the pan on high heat for about 1 minute, then lower the heat. When you're able to shake it loose, turn it out into your hand and slide it back into the pan to cook the other side. Then, using tongs, either put it on a grill, pass it over the burner of a gas stove, or hit it gently with a blowtorch to create a little char. Fill with the ingredients, and let them warm through on top of the tlayuda in the pan. A few shakes of hot sauce, and you're good to go.

TUNA TOSTADA

2 small corn tortillas
2 oz mozzarella or other melting cheese
1 small can tuna
1 tsp mayonnaise
1 small piece orange pepper, chopped
¼ C cilantro, chopped
2 quail eggs
1 tsp butter

This is a simple recipe to make very quickly, using either store-bought tortillas or freshly made. Start by passing the tortillas over a flame on both sides, then place in a large pan over low heat. Add a few bits of cheese to the tortilla to stick everything down. Then mix the drained tuna with the mayo and place little bits in the empty spaces between the cheese. Sprinkle on the chopped orange pepper, the cilantro, and a little more cheese. Then cut open the quail eggs with scissors and fry gently in another pan, in the butter. Slide these on top of the tostada. Keep checking the bottom of the tortillas; you want them crispy but not burned. Serve when the bottoms are crisp and the cheese melted. I have put all manner of ingredients on a tostada, including poached cardoons, fried salmon skin, and liverwurst. There are no holds barred on this one.

POLENTA CRISPS

These are, of course, not from Mexico, but I've included them here because aesthetically they're so similar to the other recipes in this section. The only major difference is that when Europeans encountered corn, they didn't quite understand why people soaked corn kernels in ashes or slaked lime. The process is called nixtamalization, and it not only makes the masa bouncy and causes it to hold together, it also makes available niacin. In Europe, and in the United States too, the corn was just ground. If you tried to live on this, you might end up with a vitamin deficiency disease called pellagra. In Italy specifically, corn just took the place of barley or millet in polenta after the sixteenth century.

You will have to trust me, this is not a recipe to be measured. You mess with the Maize God Chicomecōātl if you do. So just get a medium-sized pot with a heavy bottom and fill it about three-quarters full with water, and bring the water to a boil with about 2 teaspoons of salt. Gently sprinkle in 10 handfuls of polenta, stirring now and then. If you try to do this any other way, the corn sticks together in lumps. Stir again. Turn the heat down to medium-low and let cook gently about 5 minutes. Then add 2 tablespoons of butter and a few good glugs of milk—about 2 cups. Stir again, and let cook another 30 minutes. The polenta will be good to eat right now. Take about half, put it in a rectangular plastic container, and leave in the fridge until morning.

The next day slide the solid polenta block onto a wooden cutting board and slice into 1-inch-thick slabs. Heat a large, nonstick pan with 3 tablespoons of olive oil. Place the slabs in the pan, being sure they don't overlap. Cook on medium-low heat for about 15 minutes and then turn over. Cook on both sides until browned and crunchy. This will take at least half an hour. Whatever you do, don't cover them, or they'll go soggy. When ready to eat, place on paper towels to drain, if you like, or just top with whatever you like and eat.

Cheese makes perfect sense, as does a thinly sliced mound of prosciutto, or any other cold cut. If you prefer a more traditional direction, top with cream cheese and a little apricot jam.

LENTIL TORTILLA

Honestly, I was trying to make a kind of pappadam without urad dal. But a dough made of lentils is very hard to roll out, so why not press it between two sheets of plastic in a tortilla press? I tried, and it worked remarkably well. I wonder why beans aren't made this way more often. It certainly cuts down the cooking time.

¼ C French green lentils
⅛ C water
2 Tbs olive oil
1 tsp Greek yogurt

¼ C cured salmon, shredded
1 tsp capers
1 quail egg

Grind the lentils in a spice grinder, food processor, or other device until they become a fine powder. Add the water and 1 tsp of the oil. Mix into a dough, then roll into a ball and let rest, covered, about 5 minutes. Heat the rest of the oil in a nonstick pan. Press out the dough in a tortilla press and fry until lightly browned on each side. Let the tortilla drain on a paper towel. In the same pan, fry the quail egg. Put a dollop of yogurt on the tortilla, the salmon, and a few capers. Top with the egg. Of course, a regular hen's egg will be fine instead, and a dash of hot sauce wouldn't be amiss. Now that I think of it, this would be really good with sausage, too.

Lentil Tortilla

FRY BREAD WITH OCTOPUS AND FETA

This dish was invented when Native American peoples were moved onto reservations and given US government surplus provisions, such as white flour and oil. There was nothing like it in the traditional cuisines of Indigenous people, but it has nonetheless become an indispensable part of the culture, regularly served at powwows and social gatherings. Made well, it is actually not greasy at all, but soft and chewy and perfect for wrapping around ingredients. I would argue it's much tastier than a flour tortilla, but here I have pretended it was a pita bread, with astonishing results.

½ C refined, bleached white
    all-purpose flour
½ tsp baking powder
¼ tsp salt
¼ C milk

Pan with 2 inches peanut oil
2 Tbs feta cheese
½ C pea shoots
2 pieces smoked octopus

Mix the flour, baking powder, salt, and milk in a bowl and work into a firm dough. Heat the oil over a medium flame. Roll the dough into 2 rounds on a floured board. Fry them, one at a time. They will puff up dramatically. Turn over and let bubble away until light brown on both sides. Let them drain on paper towels.

Spread the feta cheese over the fry bread, sprinkle on some shoots, add the octopus, and fold in half. Consume immediately.

Fry Bread with Octopus and Feta

CHOPPED LIVER ON RYE TORTILLA

I am told that in Los Angeles there is a place that serves pastrami on a taco. I don't know whether it's a conscious act of fusion or a natural combination of ingredients resulting from the people who happen to live in proximity—like a Korean taco. I do know from personal experience that such combinations seem jarring to those not embedded in hybrid cultures, but they do happen spontaneously. What follows would probably never happen on its own, but it does follow a comment I once heard that the pastrami combination would never be complete without a rye tortilla. Here, I've gone a step further.

Chopped Liver (enough for many servings)
1 lb chicken liver
Skin and fat from a chicken
1 onion
2 eggs
1 tsp salt
¼ C port

Taco (1 serving, multiply as needed)
¼ C dark rye flour
Pinch of salt
1 Tbs olive oil
Boiling water

Garnishes
1 oz aged cheddar
Radish sprouts

Poach the livers in unsalted, simmering water for 4 or 5 minutes, until cooked through but still pink. Remove and let cool. Place the skin and fat in a pan, and render over low heat until the skin is crisp. Remove the skin and cut into small pieces. These are called *gribenes* in Yiddish. Chop the onion finely, and cook in the chicken fat with a pinch of salt. Let it cook slowly, about 15 minutes. Meanwhile, hard-boil two eggs. Chop the liver very finely and add all the other ingredients. Chill.

Mix the rye flour, salt, oil, and just enough boiling water (about 2 tablespoons) to make a soft dough. Flatten the dough between the palms of your hands, turning it around often to make sure it's even. It should be as thin as you can get it. Lay it in a hot, ungreased nonstick pan and cook until brown on both sides. Place it over an open flame to char slightly and puff up a little.

To assemble, place two scoops of chopped liver on the taco, some radish sprouts, and the cheese, broken up into small bits. Hit the cheese with a blowtorch to melt, or place under the broiler. Fold the taco and enjoy. I think this would also be nice with a little mustard, maybe a few gherkin pickles, too.

PUPUSA WITH SQUASH

I was trying to imagine what a pupusa would have been like before the Spanish arrived. That would mean no pork or cheese—not even the curtido, which is a Salvadoran slaw made of European cabbage and carrots. Joining the "three sisters"—corn, squash, and beans—together seemed to make sense, and so it makes sense on the palate as well. If you can find an American herb and souring agent other than lime, all the better.

½ C masa harina
½ C water
¼ tsp salt
¼ C roasted kabocha or other squash

Salsa
1 tomato
¼ C black beans
Few sprigs cilantro or Mexican oregano (*Lippia graveolens*)
¼ avocado
¼ tsp salt
Squirt of lime juice

The night before, chop the squash into large pieces and remove the seeds. Sprinkle with salt and a little oil or butter, perhaps a drizzle of maple syrup, and roast at 350°F for an hour. Eat the squash for dinner, but save a little leftover for the next morning. In the morning, heat a nonstick frying pan, comal, or other cooking surface without oil. Mix the masa flour, water, and salt. Roll into a ball and flatten with your fingers. Place the squash inside the disk and gently fold over the edges until the pupusa is sealed. Cook in the pan over medium heat for about 5 minutes per side or until blistered with brown spots. While that is happening, mix all the other ingredients to make a quick salsa from the Americas.

Pupusa with Squash

Stuffed Things
and Potted Meats

STUFFED THINGS

Buckwheat Jaffles

Jaffles is a term known only in Australia. In the United States I've heard them called Mountain Pies and Pudgie Pies (the brand of sandwich iron that I own). My mother called them Flying Saucers (because we had a round iron). It's two hemispherical disks connected with a hinge that closes tightly, with a smooth interior and extra long handles. "Jaffles" is an infinitely superior moniker. Normally "jaffles" means just white bread with cheese inside, cooked over an open fire or on the stove, so that it becomes an enclosed grilled cheese pie. You could add other ingredients, such as meat or even fruit. But why not make the crust itself in the iron? A regular, butter-laden crust would either burn or get too greasy from the cheese inside. I like the idea of using masa or raw tortilla dough, which works very nicely, but so does buckwheat. For this, you need a fine, light buckwheat flour, not whole ground buckwheat groats (kasha), which won't hold together. If you're in doubt, mix a pinch of the buckwheat flour with a little water; it should become a sticky dough immediately.

> ½ C light, hulled buckwheat flour
> ¼–⅓ C water
> Pinch of salt
> 2 tsp salted butter
> 2 slices prosciutto
> ½ C young pecorino (not hard, aged pecorino Romano), shredded
> 1 Tbs fennel seed

Mix the buckwheat flour with the water and salt, and work into a smooth dough that's not too sticky. You might need to add a little more flour. Divide it into two balls. Grease the inside of your jaffle iron generously with the butter. There should be a lot—it will seep into the dough, making it crisp; without it, the pastry would be hard and inedible. Flatten the balls, and press them into each side of the iron, all the way to the edges, so you have thin layers with no holes. If there's extra dough on the edges, don't worry. Shred the cheese, and add half to one side of the iron. Chop the prosciutto fine and add it on top. Then add the rest of the cheese. Chop the fennel fine (rather than pound in a mortar) and add that. Close the other side so the dough encloses the ingredients. With a knife, cut off any excess that squishes out the sides. Place on low heat and cook for 10 minutes, turning frequently. Put on a plate and serve.

Buckwheat Jaffles

Cajun Shrimp Toast with Rémoulade

When I was young we used to go to a tiki-themed Chinese restaurant that did the notorious "pu-pu platter." It was a rotating wooden tower of kebabs with pineapple, chicken in little tinfoil triangles, pork dumplings, and my favorite: shrimp toast. This was a piece of plain white bread smeared with shrimp paste (basically stuffing) and deep-fried, so that it was crisp and greasy. Not long ago, I was up late one night thinking how this might be improved. What if you used really good bread, flavored the shrimp paste more intensely, and instead of frying, just sautéed it in a little butter in a pan? Make it easy? I was about to make a traditional Chinese shrimp filling with ginger, scallions, and sesame oil, and then the can of Old Bay stared right back at me. The rest of the ingredients simply fell in line, beautifully. If you don't see this on the menu at a fast-casual joint in the near future, the management is clearly sleeping on the job. It is that good.

1 slice sourdough bread
1 handful peeled raw shrimp
1 dash each of Old Bay, salt, pepper, coriander, oregano, cayenne pepper
1 Tbs red onion, chopped
1 tsp cornstarch
1 Tbs butter

Rémoulade
1 Tbs mayonnaise
5 dashes of Louisiana smoked chipotle hot sauce
1 dash Worcestershire sauce
Few drops lemon juice
1 Tbs capers

Toast the bread lightly. With a cleaver, chop the shrimp thoroughly until they stick together and form a smooth and solid paste. Mix in the seasonings, onion, and cornstarch. Spread the toast evenly with the shrimp paste. Heat the butter in a nonstick pan, and fry the toast face-down until browned. Turn over and cook the bread side, too.

Make the sauce by mixing all the ingredients, then just drizzle over the shrimp toast. Sprinkle with a little more Old Bay before serving.

Cajun Shrimp Toast with Rémoulade

Stuffed Tofu

I understand that some people are less than thrilled by the prospect of eating tofu. I believe that's primarily because it has been presented as a substitute for meat, when it's not even vaguely like meat. Others say that it has no flavor, or depends on seasoning for interest. I disagree. Fresh tofu can be exquisite. I've eaten soft, almost evanescent tofu in Japan with no condiments at all, and it was extraordinarily flavorful. That's not the tofu we can get in the supermarket, alas. I've made it from scratch a few times, too, and although it worked well enough, I think that unless you have perfectly fresh beans and a lot of experience, you should buy what you can. So admittedly, I do fry it, season it, and in this case, pack it with a punch that will convince even the most ardent doubters that it can be lovely. The idea comes from a Taiwanese Hakka dish usually made with ground pork.

> 1 rectangle extra-firm tofu about the size of the palm of your hand
> 4 Tbs canola oil
> 2 Tbs soy sauce
> 1 Tbs balsamic vinegar or Chinese black vinegar
> 1 small sausage
> 1 very small potato
> A handful of greens, such as kale, broccoli rabe, or collards

Dry off the tofu with paper towels. Heat the oil in a nonstick skillet, and fry the tofu gently on all sides. It will sputter and spew hot oil, so stand back. Brown both sides, as well as the edges, by standing the block on each side in turn. It takes a little time but is so much easier than deep-frying. Then place on a dry paper towel to drain off some of the oil. Place in a bowl and marinate with the soy and vinegar. Then put the sausage, chopped potato, and greens in the pan. Keep them in separate corners and cook through, about 10 minutes. Slice the sausage into rounds.

Cut a slit in the side of the tofu and stuff in the sausage and other fillings, being careful not to split the tofu. You might not be able to fit everything inside. Then cut it diagonally and continue to cook with the cut side down. You might need to add another spot of oil. This will make everything crisp and allow the flavors to meld. Serve like a sandwich.

Stuffed Tofu

Migas

I believe that when you allow your creative energy to flow, you may start with a particular idea for a recipe, but an invisible force leads you elsewhere. When the idea strikes you to take the dish in a different direction, just allow it to happen. Do you feel like changing course again? Go ahead. It's very much like wandering with no particular destination in mind—something I do often. Those are always the best walks, especially when it's a city I don't know. It's exactly the same with cooking. I started off wanting to make migas—look where I ended up.

To start, there are two very different kinds of migas. One is Mexican and is based on tortillas; the original is from Spain and made from stale bread. I had plenty of stale bread around, so I used that. I began by cooking off a little pancetta in a pan, then chopped some red onion and added that. Measurements would be ridiculous in this case—just use about equal quantities of the ingredients you add.

Dice 1 stalk of celery and 1 small carrot, and add those. Add 3 or 4 brown mushrooms, chopped. (This is just what I found while rooting around in the fridge.) But wait, how is migas different from stuffing? Not much. So what if I threw in some sage now? And just added the little bits of torn stale bread, fried them all together, and then moistened with about half a cup of chicken stock, tossing gently so the bread doesn't break up? The result is a quick stuffing.

But how can I stop there? Thanksgiving is looming on the horizon. The first taste of cooler weather where I live in California. Wrap the stuffing in a slice of deli roasted turkey. Wrap that in a Vietnamese rice paper wrapper. The flavors and textures go magnificently together. Just the right size for a nosh, too. There's no need for sauce, but I suppose a little fish sauce, lime, green onion, and cranberry couldn't hurt.

Migas

Steamed Buns with Bratwurst and Kraut

The dough for this recipe is more or less the same as for pizza and pita bread, but the texture when steamed comes out more like a chewy pretzel. A friend suggested I should call these baotzels. I suggest making two small, thin pizzas for dinner one night and saving one-third of the dough for two steamed buns in the morning. You might think this is a complicated process that takes a long time, but seriously, the assembly takes just a few minutes, and the steaming itself about 20 minutes. You can make the sauerkraut yourself about a week ahead or use store-bought.

Kraut
1 head cabbage
2 Tbs sea salt (without iodine)
A few sprigs dill, or caraway seed, if desired

Cut the cabbage in quarters through the bottom and remove the core. Then slice each quarter thinly. Place in a large bowl, sprinkle with the salt, and massage until the water starts coming out of the cabbage. Stuff the cabbage and its liquid into some 2 pint jars and seal the lids. The liquid should come right to the top. Place on the counter, and every day just loosen the lid a little to let out the gas. After a week it should be pleasantly sour and still crunchy.

Dough
1 packet yeast
1 C water at 110°F
Pinch of sugar
About 3 C flour
1 tsp salt

Mix the yeast with the hot water and sugar until it activates and gets frothy. Add the flour slowly, while stirring. Then add the salt. Knead for about 5 minutes. Place in a bowl and let rise for about an hour, covered with a dishcloth.

Making the Buns
2 lumps of dough
1 small bratwurst (precooked)
2 Tbs sauerkraut
1 tsp toasted sesame oil
¼ tsp each white and black sesame seeds

Take two lumps of dough the size of your fist and roll them on a well-floured wooden board into rounds. Place about 1 tablespoon of kraut on the dough and cover with half of a small, precooked bratwurst sausage. You can also use a section of kielbasa or other smoked sausage. Dab on some mustard. Then fold the dough over the filling by lifting over an edge and moving around the circle, lifting over just a small bit of dough at a time, so you have a sort of skirt edge pleating. Pinch the top closed.

Place your buns on a piece of parchment paper, put into a steamer, and steam over boiling water for 20 minutes. Remove the buns and rub them with sesame oil and sprinkle on the seeds. If you like, pass a blowtorch over the top briefly to toast the seeds.

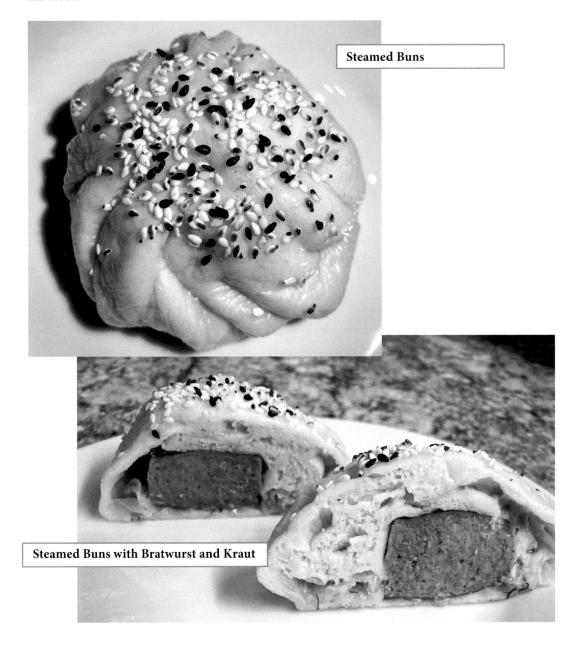

Steamed Buns

Steamed Buns with Bratwurst and Kraut

Boyos

"My grandma was the best cook ever!" says anyone who has ever been interested in cooking and eating. I say the same thing myself. For years, I have been trying to replicate my grandmother's recipes from memory. She died when I was thirteen, so it's mostly guesswork. One of these recipes is boyos—a kind of round roll with spinach and feta filling. There were also other fillings, like onion and egg, ground beef too. I recall vividly one day exclaiming how much I liked them, so whenever I saw her, she would have made dozens just for me, to put in the freezer and have for breakfast every day. In all honesty, they were a bit dense, and as she was Mediterranean at heart, she poured olive oil on top. My father would become incensed; he liked them fine without oil, but she insisted. Oil or otherwise, they are the perfect noshing food.

After a little sleuthing I found that "boyoz," as it is spelled in Turkey, are still made in the city of Izmir (Smyrna) where my grandmother's family came from, and they are still associated with the Sephardic Jewish community. The Spanish name is *bollos,* and they do come originally from Spain. In Turkey, they are often unfilled and are made of a pulled filo dough, light like a croissant. Nothing like my grandmother's boyos.

For this recipe I thought about how much better boyos would be if light and flaky, so I made a simple, yeasted and laminated croissant-like dough with butter. I also used broccoli rabe instead of spinach, because the oxalic acid in the spinach strips the enamel off my teeth and makes them feel chalky—and also because rabe is the best vegetable on earth, period. Use a good creamy feta, too, ideally from Bulgaria, but French feta can also be great.

1 C pastry flour
⅛ tsp sea salt
1 tsp instant yeast
⅓ C water, plus a little more for kneading
6 Tbs salted butter
1 bunch broccoli rabe
3 Tbs olive oil
1 tsp salt
6 oz feta cheese
1 egg
1 tsp each black and white sesame seeds

Mix the flour, salt, yeast, and water, and knead for about 10 minutes, keeping your hands wet with extra water (rather than dry with flour). Place pats of the cold butter, neatly aligned and touching, on a sheet of plastic wrap and put another sheet on top. Roll it out into a thin contiguous square. Roll out the dough on a large wooden board, this time floured. Remove the top sheet of plastic from the butter and set it directly on the dough; then remove the other sheet. Fold the dough over the butter like a book and roll out. Repeat folding over and rolling out 4 or 5 times more, then wrap the dough in the plastic and let rest in the fridge for an hour.

Chop the broccoli rabe, discarding the thick ends of the stems. Fry it in the oil and season with salt. Cook over medium heat, stirring now and then, for about 15 minutes. Remove from the pan and place in a bowl to cool. Then crumble in the feta and add ¾ of the egg. Mix well. Set aside until the dough is finished resting in the fridge.

Roll out the dough on a floured board. Cut into four pieces. Place the filling in the center of each piece and fold over the sides, encasing the filling. Then turn them over, so the top is smooth. Brush with the remaining egg and sprinkle with sesame seeds.

Then heat the oven to 400°F. Bake the boyos for 10 minutes and then lower the heat to 350°F and cook another 20 minutes until browned. Eat them hot.

Boyos

Alternative Tamales

Most people consider tamales extremely labor-intensive, requiring a whole day and an army of relatives and neighbors to assemble. Well, so they are—if you are making hundreds. For a few, they are quick to assemble. Tamales do take a long time to steam, but that's entirely passive cooking. Just pop a small batch in the fridge and reheat through the week as needed. These are utterly untraditional, a cross between a tamal and a kind of little steamed English pudding, though not sweet. The key is beating the fat—preferably lard—into a fluffy mass before adding the other ingredients. You could use suet or duck fat instead, but olive oil doesn't work well. I have had the best results with chickpea flour and oat flour, something with a slightly coarse grind, but definitely not groats or grits. Teff is nice and so is benne flour, which is a kind of sesame seed with the oil removed.

    3 corn husks
    1 Tbs lard
    ½ C chickpea flour
    ½ tsp baking soda
    ¼ tsp salt
    ⅛ tsp smoked paprika
    ⅛ tsp cayenne
    ¼ C buttermilk

Start by soaking the corn husks. Multiply the recipe for the number of tamales you want; these measurements are for a single serving of two. Beat the lard with a wooden spoon in a small bowl until fluffy. Add all the other ingredients in order, and then continue beating. Spread out the corn husks, divide the dough in two, and spread on two of the husks. Fold over the bottom end, then the sides, then the pointy end of each husk, so the filling is completely encased. Rip a strip from the remaining husk and tie the tamales shut. Place in a steaming basket and steam for 1 ½ hours. If you have a small basket, you'll need to refill the water several times. It's better to have a big tamal steamer or a large aluminum one used for Asian dumplings. A bamboo steamer works fine, too. With a big steamer, you can make 8 or 10 tamales and use a different filling in each one. You can also put other fillings inside, encased in the dough. A puree of beans or braised meat is ideal. But I find it easier to serve on the side with the tamales.

Stuffed Flatbread

This flatbread is an unusual kind of dough, made from semolina flour, that gets its delicacy from stretching. It's something like filo or strudel dough, but much easier to manage in small pieces. Also, it is cooked in a pan on the stovetop, so it is quite quick to prepare. The only essential trick requiring a little patience is kneading the dough and letting it rest overnight. Once you get up in the morning, it only takes a few minutes to assemble.

Dough	Filling
1 C semolina flour	1 C shredded mozzarella
1 bowl of water	1 C crumbly cheese, such as
1 tsp salt	cotija, feta, or white
2 Tbs olive oil	1 C cilantro, chopped

Place the flour in a bowl and the water beside it. Start by sprinkling in the water with one hand and pinching and crushing the dough with the other. Keep sprinkling in the water until the flour comes together as a dough. Move the dough to a wooden board to knead.

Dip both your hands in the water and wring off the excess. Knead the dough, and every now and then dip your hands back in the water and wring them off. You'll see that the water becomes cloudy with starch. What you are doing is removing some of the starch that sticks to your hands, which increases the protein by volume in the dough, making it more stretchy. Knead and continue adding the water that clings to your hands for about 5 minutes. By then you'll have a super-smooth and elastic dough. Divide it into four balls. Place the oil on a plate and roll the balls around in it. Flatten them into disks and cover with plastic wrap. Leave them overnight to rest.

The next morning, mix your filling. You can actually add anything you like. I have tried it with leftover barbecued pork, and it was delicious. Walnuts and some urfa chili flakes with cheese were also delightful.

There are a few ways you can fold in the ingredients. First, roll out one disk of the dough into a wide circle on a wooden board. Then carefully stretch the edges so the circle becomes bigger and bigger. It should be about the size of a big dinner plate and paper-thin. Then line up the cheese and herbs on one side of the dough, and roll it up into a thin snake. Pinch the ends closed, and then coil the snake into a tight spiral and press down flat. Repeat with the other disks of dough. Then cook them in an ungreased pan over medium heat, turning now and then until brown on both sides. The cheese will get all gooey inside.

You can also place the filling in the middle and fold over the edges in five or six folds until the filling is encased. Or you can just fold over two opposite sides, turn over and fold over the other sides, making a square. This way the top and bottom are of even thickness. It really doesn't matter how you fold it up. The dough is paradoxically both crisp on the outside and chewy.

If you are feeling really adventuresome, cook these rounds open (not folded in half) like a pita bread—just place it in a very hot pan for 30 seconds, then on the other side for 30 seconds. Then place it directly over an open flame and it will puff up. Keep turning it over with tongs, so it doesn't burn on one side. Then place it back in the pan to get really crisp. You can sprinkle with parmesan cheese and chopped herbs, or even sugar and cinnamon.

Stuffed Flatbread

Chicken Pot Pie

This is an old favorite, updated, and a great way to use up leftover roast chicken. The key to a really crisp bottom crust—for no one likes a soggy bottom—is to use more butter than you think possible to meld with flour, and then don't let the filling be wet, either. For this, I used two small, oval nonstick tart pans, though you can, of course, make one, or many more. They freeze well, too. To serve, I took it out of the tart pan for dramatic effect.

Crust
4 Tbs salted butter
½ C whole wheat pastry flour
Less than ¼ C cold water

Filling
1 C leftover roasted chicken, skin and bones removed
1 scallion, sliced
1 small carrot
¼ C peas
5 fresh sage leaves, chopped
1 sprig rosemary, stem discarded, leaves chopped
1 Tbs flour

In a mixing bowl combine the cold butter with the flour using your fingers. Squish all the bits of butter as best you can and as quickly as you can. Pour in the water slowly and incorporate using your other hand. The moment it begins to come together as a dough, stop, wrap in plastic, and put it in the fridge. Don't worry if there are still globs of butter; that's what you want. Heat the oven to 350°F.

Shred the chicken and mix in all the other ingredients for the filling. Then divide the dough into four pieces,roll them into balls, and flatten. Generously dust a wooden board with flour, and roll out the balls into ovals or whatever shape fits your tart pans. Put an oval at the bottom of each pan, running up and over the sides, add filling, and cover with the remaining ovals of dough. Roll the edges under themselves, pinching the two sheets closed, creating an even, thick ridge all the way around. Then crimp the edges by pressing your right index finger on the inside of the ridge and the index and thumb of your left hand on the outside on either side of your index finger. Move your fingers together so you pinch a little curve and repeat, continuing all the way around. I like to do it again, pinching the curves so they become pointy—it just adds to the surface area and crunch. Bake about 30 minutes or until crust looks lightly browned. Slide out of the pans and serve at once, hot, on a plate. A little Branston Pickle goes very nicely.

Samosa-like Pockets

I ado not call these samosas, because there's nothing like them in India, but I acknowledge the inspiration from this ancient and highly revered cuisine. It was actually the first cuisine I ever set out to learn as best I could from books in the 1980s, and both Julie Sahni and Madhur Jaffrey were absolutely inspiring and continue to be so to this day. And I must not forget the great historian K. T. Achaya. I pray that this mash-up will not prove me an errant disciple.

Dough
½ C whole wheat pastry flour
1 Tbs butter
⅛ tsp salt
⅛ tsp ground caraway seed

Filling
1 C cooked sweet potato
⅛ tsp salt
Pinch each of ginger, ground mustard seed, turmeric, paprika
½ C frozen peas
½ C leftover tri-tip steak
24 oz peanut oil

Sauce
1 Tbs tamarind paste
Hot water
1 Tbs fresh ginger
Pinch each of ground pepper, cayenne, salt, sugar

Create your tri-tip leftovers the night before you plan to make this. Poke the raw steak all over with a paring knife on both sides to break up the fibrous strands. Marinate at least a few hours in soy, mirin, and fig balsamic vinegar. Grill until medium rare and slice thinly. That's for dinner, of course. The next day, chop half a cup of the leftover steak into little bits, then proceed with the recipe.

Put all the ingredients for the dough into a mixing bowl, work in the butter with your fingers, and add about ¼ cup of water. Knead into a smooth and firm dough, wrap in plastic, and set aside. Peel 1 small sweet potato and either boil until soft or microwave about 5 minutes. Press through a ricer or mash thoroughly, and add the spices.

Start heating your oil in a small pot over a medium flame. Roll the dough on a floured board into a circle a little bigger than your hand. Cut the dough in half. Moisten your finger and run it all along the straight-cut side of one piece of dough. Fold over one of the straight sides to form a cone and press the edge to seal. With the cone in one hand, add the meat, peas, and sweet potato and seal the curved edge, enclosing the contents. Repeat with the other piece of dough. Place the samosa-like pockets gently into the oil and fry, turning over now and then until browned, just a few minutes. Remove with a slotted spoon and place on paper towels for the oil to drain off.

Then mix the tamarind paste with enough hot water to dissolve it, and work it with your fingers until you can remove the seeds and fibers. Discard those. Grate the fresh ginger right in and add the other seasonings. By now the pocket will have cooled. Serve with the sauce. It's like a whole meal in a pocket.

Samosa-like Pockets

Chile Relleno

When I was growing up on the East Coast in the 1970s and 1980s, there were few Mexican restaurants apart from chains like El Torito and Chi-Chi's. They were places for sweet frozen margaritas and chips with dip, or if you had a meal, it was all basically the same taco or burrito with choice of meat, rice, and refried beans. So it was not until I moved west that I tasted chile relleno. The traditional version from Puebla is wonderful, though I've seen many variations, sometimes with meat. The combination of goat cheese and cottage cheese is pleasantly tangy without being overwhelming, but you can use any kind of cheese inside.

2 poblano chilies	1 egg white
½ C fresh goat cheese	½ C fine cornmeal
½ C cottage cheese	¼ C olive oil
¼ C walnuts, crushed	

Place the chilies over a flame and char all sides completely. A blowtorch works really well, too. Place the charred chilies in a paper bag for about 10 minutes, and then remove the char with your fingers. Don't wash it off. Then cut the chili on one side and remove the seeds, keeping it whole as best you can. Mix the cheeses and walnuts, and stuff each chili. Dip the stuffed chili first in the egg white and then in cornmeal. Fry them gently in the oil. Although nontraditional, the contrast of the hot melted cheese and a fresh salsa made with a chopped tomato, green onion, some black beans, and lime juice is wonderful.

Chile Relleno

Spring Pancakes (Chunbing)

Of course, these are not pancakes at all, but a kind of wrapper more closely related to a hot-water noodle dough, used for making dumplings. But they are so easy to make, and so satisfyingly chewy, that I see no reason not to make a pair and fill them with whatever cold cuts and sauce you have on hand. In the past I've used cold duck, ham, and turkey, but the filling given here really does the trick. Any kind of chutney will work. I used a cherry chutney made locally.

¼ C bread flour
Pinch of salt
¼ C boiling water
¼ tsp toasted sesame oil
Thin slices boar salami
1 tsp cherry chutney
1 radicchio leaf

Put the flour in a mixing bowl, add the salt, and pour on the boiling water. Mix with a fork, and when you can get your fingers in the mix, start kneading it into a smooth ball. This dough does not need to rest. Roll it into two balls and flatten them. Anoint them with the oil. Press the two disks together and roll the pair out on a board without any flour, into the thinnest round shape you can. If you use a tapered rolling pin and just lift the dough off the board now and then, you'll find this is a really easy dough to work with. Then cook them, still stuck together, in a dry nonstick skillet on both sides over a very low flame. You don't want these to brown at all, just cook through. They will puff up a bit in the middle. Flip them over a few times. And when the dough becomes whitish, they're done, about 3–4 minutes. Remove from the pan, and separate the two paper-thin disks—but be careful, as hot steam will pour out. Fill them with the other ingredients, roll up tightly, and enjoy.

You can also double the ratio of ingredients and make one really big pancake. On a whim I filled such a beast with grilled eggplant, sautéed broccoli rabe, and feta. I wrapped it up tightly, poured on a sauce of sesame tahini and yogurt thinned with a little milk, and then garnished with radish sprouts. The alluring combination of flavors was simply mesmerizing.

Spring Pancakes (Chunbing)

POTTED MEATS

I know people are sometimes afraid of things like Spam in a can, but they can be very good if made with care. Originally, these were simply economical ways to use the spare parts of animals before the industrial age. Like sausages and hams, these preserved products meant nothing went to waste, and I think human beings actually evolved to prefer these flavors to fresh meat, which was eaten infrequently. With the advent of refrigeration and supply chains, fresh meat became more common, and we forgot these traditional techniques, but they all make wonderful nosherei.

First is scrapple, which will be familiar to anyone in the Philadelphia area. It's normally organ meats and scraps bound with cornmeal. You cut off a slice of the loaf and fry it—exquisite. I've taken the term "scraps" literally in my house, and since I don't slaughter a pig and have guts around, I used the contents of my freezer to make a kind of meatloaf-scrapple without the offal. Then come rillettes, likewise made with leftovers, in this case goose, and I did prevent anything from going to waste since I used every part, including the honk. Finally, a spin on headcheese, made without the head, so it's more of a pork aspic. In Germany, they call it *sülze* and in Russia *kholodetz*.

Multicolor Meatloaf Scrapple

¼ lb each ground beef, turkey, lamb, chicken, sausage	1 tbs sage
	1 Tbs cayenne pepper
1 egg	1 tsp thyme
1 C panko bread crumbs	1 tsp Old Bay seasoning

If you regularly make burgers of different kinds of meat, you may very well find little odds and ends frozen, as I did one day. Defrost all five, and place in separate bowls. Divide the egg, crumbs, and seasoning among the bowls, and mix each well. Get a small loaf pan or baking dish. Make a thin layer of the first meat and then continue with all the rest so you have five thin patties forming distinct layers. Cover with a piece of parchment paper pressed close to the surface and bake for about 40 minutes at 350°F. Then cool and place in the refrigerator overnight or up to a few days. Unmold, and slice off a few 1 inch pieces. Fry them. Serve on toast with mustard or along with eggs. By pure chance, the stripes make it look like bacon.

Goose Rillettes

1 goose, about 10–12 lbs	2 large onions
Salt and pepper	2 carrots
5 stalks celery	1 tsp each fennel, thyme, salt, and pepper
1 C goose fat	
2 C goose stock	1 C port

Begin by seasoning the goose simply with salt and pepper, and letting rest a day or so in the fridge. Bring it to room temperature, prick the skin all over with a skewer, and bake in a deep roasting pan on top of the celery at 350°F for 2 ½ hours. Remove the fat with a baster or deep spoon and save in a container in the fridge. You should get 4 cups or so from a domestic bird. Remove the goose from the oven and let rest 45 minutes. Eat the goose for dinner.

I usually have a few pints of goose stock in the freezer from the last goose I cooked, for exactly such occasions as this. Making the stock is very simple. Strip the carcass of meat, and throw it in a large stockpot with the wings, neck, and giblets. Add aromatics, such as an onion, celery, carrot, sprigs of thyme. Cover with water and let simmer slowly for at least 12 hours. Strain through cheesecloth into a smaller pot and reduce by half on low heat, for about 1 hour or more. Set aside a cup of this and freeze the rest. Or, of course, make fresh stock from the goose you just had for dinner.

Naturally, you will have leftover meat. Use about 3 cups of the meat, and the stock and fat you have set aside. Shred the meat and cook in 2 tablespoons of the fat. Add 1 onion, chopped, and let that brown well with the goose. Add in the seasonings. Cook for about 15 minutes, then add the stock and the port. Let simmer, breaking up the goose meat into fine shreds. When all the liquid is absorbed, place the meat in a glass canning jar and press down. I used a single, large Weck container, but you can also use several smaller ones. I like that the lids on Weck jars are glass and won't rust. Just make sure the contents completely fill the jar. Pour melted goose fat over the meat until it comes right up to the top, and put the lid on. Place in the fridge and let it become solid and ripen for a few days. When you're ready to nosh, scoop out a spoonful and spread on warm toast.

Goose Rilletes

Pork Aspic, or Headless Headcheese

In the wake of writing a book on aspic, I didn't think I would touch the stuff again, but I couldn't resist making this one. If you have an aversion to pig's foot, this can be made with packages of unflavored gelatin. And if you like very firm headcheese, the kind you can slice and put on a sandwich, then you can add a little extra gelatin, too. Just be sure to dissolve the gelatin in cool liquid first, following the package directions, before adding it to hot liquid.

> 1 pork shoulder chop
> 1 tsp salt
> ½ tsp sugar
> ⅛ tsp Insta Cure #1
> 1 pig's foot, split
> 1 shallot
> 1 stalk celery
> 1 carrot
> 1 tsp whole pepper corns
> 1 tsp salt
> ¼ C apple cider vinegar

First, remove the meat from the pork chop, saving the bone. Cut into small cubes, and add the salt, sugar, and curing salt. Put in a plastic bag and keep in the refrigerator at least one day.

Then put the pig's foot, pork chop bone, shallot, celery, carrot, salt and pepper, and vinegar into a pot and simmer on low for about 6 hours. Or cook in an instant pot or pressure cooker under high pressure for 90 minutes. Strain into a container, and put the container into the fridge—or, in winter, leave it outside overnight. In the morning, scrape off any fat from the top. Beneath, the liquid should be lightly set as a jelly. Reheat and strain if necessary to remove any particles, and then reduce by half over gentle heat—giving you about 2 cups. This is the point when you would add extra gelatin if you want it really bouncy. Or the point when you just mix some flavorful broth with gelatin and skip the foot entirely.

Place the cubed meat in a glass canning jar. Pour the hot gelatin over this. Cover the jar and put it into a pot of simmering water; cook for about 15 minutes, or until you see the meat has cooked through. Remove from the water, let cool on the counter, and then place in the fridge until solidified. When you're ready to eat it, just run under warm water, slice the jelly out onto a board, slice, and eat cold. Or, if you prefer, just scoop out the jelly by the spoonful, which is easier if it's loosely set. Serve with mustard and pickles, naturally.

Pork Aspic, or Headless Headcheese

Pancakes and Variations

OKONOMI WAFFLE

In Japan you can find these big, honking savory pancakes that are eaten much the way Americans eat pizza, late at night. Scaled down, they also make a great snack. I stayed vaguely within the boundaries of those commonly eaten, though keep in mind the name itself means "as you like it," so there really are no rules. The only significant difference is that I used a waffle iron.

1 C cabbage, finely chopped
1 tsp salt
1 C okonomiyaki flour (found in Japanese groceries)
1 C Bulgarian cultured buttermilk or regular buttermilk
2 slices Prosciutto di San Daniele
1 tsp butter
Okonomi sauce in a squirt bottle
Kewpie mayonnaise in a squirt bottle
2 Tbs red capelin roe (masago)

Salt the cabbage, and massage well until it releases water. Squeeze and discard as much water as you can. Add the okonomiyaki flour; regular pancake batter or a commercial mix will work, too. Then add the buttermilk, and stir until you have a thick batter. Roll up the prosciutto and cut into fine ribbons. Add that to the batter and stir in. Heat your waffle iron and grease with butter. Pour in the batter without pressing down too hard. When cooked, plate the waffles, squirt on the sauce and mayo in fine lines, and strew with the roe.

Okonomi Waffle

IDLI WITH ALMOND BUTTER
AND PERSIMMON CHUTNEY

Were I to tell you that this recipe is highly reminiscent of a peanut butter and jelly sandwich, you probably wouldn't believe me, but it's true. Idli, from southern India, are soft, cakey rounds that are oddly like white bread but pleasantly sour and made entirely from fermented rice and beans. Almond butter is more nuanced than peanut, but either would work well, and the chutney is infinitely more vibrant than jelly. Combining these ingredients came to me entirely serendipitously. About a decade ago I planted a little persimmon tree at the corner of my house, where it received next to no light and even less water. I vaguely remembered it was there, but it never bore fruit and never grew. Recently we trimmed back nearby trees and fixed the sprinkler. I happened to be poking around in front of the house mid-October, and what did I find? Three gorgeous fuyu persimmons, crisp and sweet and ready to go on the idli I had just steamed.

This recipe is delicious, unusual, and quick. The only thing you need to start ahead of time is the batter, but it takes very little effort.

Idli
2 C basmati rice
½ C urad dal (tiny white black gram beans with the outer coating removed—not lentils)
Spring water or filtered tap water
½ Tbs butter
1 Tbs almond butter

Put the rice in one large bowl and the beans in another. Barely cover each with water. Cover with a dishcloth and allow them to ferment for 2 days. Next, put them together in a blender and process until smooth and the consistency of cream. Return to a single large bowl and cover. Let ferment another 2 days, stirring a few times each day. Don't be alarmed by any errant aromas the bowl may emit. It cannot go bad. It's simply adjusting to your local environment, and the lactobacilli are multiplying, fending off other bacteria. At this point it should be frothy and thick and resemble whipped egg whites. If your house is hot, it may go quicker; the opposite, if cold.

Generously butter a small bowl about 4 inches in diameter and pour in some batter, about half way up. Place the bowl into a steamer and cook for 12 minutes. A smaller bowl will take a little less time, a larger one, a bit more. Remove from the steamer and let cool for a few minutes. Run a knife around the perimeter to loosen the idli and turn out onto a board. Slice the idli horizontally so you have a top and bottom, like a little bun. Spread the almond butter on one side.

Persimmon Chutney
2 Tbs neutral oil such as vegetable, corn or canola
1 small shallot
1 knob of ginger
1 small fuyu persimmon
About 20 golden raisins
1 Tbs vinegar

When you put your idli in to steam, peel and chop the shallot and start to cook gently in the oil. Peel the ginger with a spoon, slice and dice finely, then add to the pan. Chop the persimmon finely and add. Chop the raisins finely and add them. Splash with vinegar. Ideally this should be cooked just enough by the time your idli are done, about 12 minutes. Or let cook a few minutes longer if necessary. Put a good dollop of the chutney on top of the almond butter, close, and serve just as you would a PB&J sandwich.

Idli with Almond Butter and Persimmon Chutney

SAVORY BLINTZ

Part of me wanted to call this a crespella or crepe; all thin pancakes are ultimately related. Historically, the Italian and French versions were baked into a thin wafer over an open fire in an iron mold or fried in fat until crisp, and our English word "crisp" comes from the dish. But now they're more like big, thin pancakes wrapped around fillings. This is really more of a blintz, and in the interest of a weekday time schedule, I made it as quickly as possible.

⅓ C all-purpose flour
1 large egg
¼ C buttermilk
¼ C water
2 Tbs butter
½ C cottage cheese
¼ C crumbled blue cheese
2 slices mortadella

Dump the first 4 ingredients in a bowl and mix. Gently melt the butter in a large nonstick pan. Pour half that butter into the batter and swirl the rest around. Crank up your heat to high and pour the batter into the pan, swirling around so it covers the entire surface. Turn down the heat. Cook on one side for about 3 minutes, then flip over. Move the pancake to a big plate with the first cooked side down. Put all the other ingredients inside and roll up tightly, tucking in the ends before you finish rolling up. Put back in the pan and cook until it is brown on all sides and the cheese is melted. Cut in half and serve. Add any cold cuts, and any cheese works wonderfully, too.

HOECAKES WITH PEANUT, PORK CRACKLINGS, AND SHRIMP OR CHARRED PERSIMMON SALSA

I love the fanciful story that hoecakes were cooked over hot coals on the blade of a garden hoe. But alas, no. The "hoe" is the iron pan. Hoecakes are a cousin to johnnycake and corn pone, or corn bread. The cornmeal used is of paramount importance here. I used Marsh Hen Mill cornmeal, very finely ground.

1 ¼ C fine cornmeal
¼ tsp baking soda
½ tsp sea salt
1 Tbs peanut powder (defatted)

½ C buttermilk
1 Tbs peanut oil
½ beaten egg
1 handful crushed pork cracklings
Pinch of cayenne powder
1 Tbs butter

7 peeled shrimp
¼ tsp Old Bay seasoning

1 Tbs sorghum syrup
1 Tbs Bulleit Bourbon

Mix the cornmeal, baking soda, salt, and peanut powder in a bowl. In another bowl, mix the milk, oil, and egg. Give the other half of the egg to the dog. Mix the contents of the two bowls together and add pork rinds and cayenne. Melt the butter in a cast-iron pan, and fry the batter over medium heat. You can make one large cake or a few small ones; flip over when browned. Then sprinkle the Old Bay on the shrimp, leaving the tails on, if you like. Fry in the same pan, and arrange on top of the cakes. Then mix the syrup and bourbon, and place in a small bowl on the side.

   If you'd rather not make shrimp, this charred persimmon salsa also goes very well with the cakes.

Charred Persimmon Salsa
1 small fuyu persimmon (small, squat, hard kind)
½ red bell pepper
1 scallion
1 inch piece ginger
Splash of rice wine vinegar
¼ tsp salt

Place your persimmon directly over a gas flame. If you have a blowtorch, that works wonderfully, too. Char the fruit until completely blackened. Place in a paper bag, close, and let it steam for a few minutes. Then scrape off the char. Don't rinse. Chop into cubes. Chop up the other ingredients and add them, too, with the vinegar and salt. You can ramp this recipe up for any number of persimmons, naturally.

Hoecakes with Peanut, Pork Cracklings, and Shrimp or Charred Persimmon Salsa

FISH PUPPIES

I spent an inordinate amount of time thinking of a cute name for these, longer than it took to cook them, and finally this name was offered by a friend on Facebook. It doesn't capture the corn-dog-on-a-stick aspect, but it's delightful all the same. Make these when you have leftover oil from cooking the night before, still sitting on the stove in the morning. Or if you prefer, heat a quart of oil and make a big batch by multiplying the ingredients.

1 C fine cornmeal	3 small wedges salmon,
1 tsp baking powder	about an ounce each
½ C buttermilk	1 qt peanut oil
½ tsp sea salt	Squirt of Kewpie mayo

Heat the oil over medium heat. Mix the cornmeal, baking powder, buttermilk, and salt. Add more liquid if necessary to get a thick batter. Test the oil with a drop of batter. If it floats up, it's ready. Dip the fish in the batter, coating it completely, and gently slide into the oil. Cook until golden brown. Drain on paper towels. If you like, serve on a wooden skewer with a squirt of mayo.

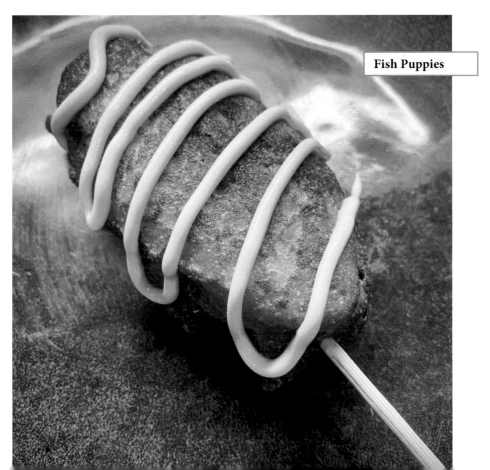

Fish Puppies

INJERA

When I lived in Washington, DC, there was a fabulous Ethiopian restaurant in the Adams-Morgan neighborhood. If you showed even the slightest sign of hesitation over how to deal with a large, flat pancake laden with globs of food, the server would grab a pinch themself and say, "Let me feed you," and stuff it in your mouth. Being fed by another person is such an act of intimacy that your guard was immediately let down and you were placed at ease with the thought of having to use your fingers. It is said that one-third of the world uses cutlery, one-third chopsticks, and one-third fingers. It's a shame that so many of us hesitate to eat with our fingers. It brings you closer to the food, and allows you to interact with it more directly and, I believe, appreciate it more fully. I actually had a friend in college who only ate with her fingers. She was a stunningly beautiful hippie named Jessica. No one would sit with her while she ate and stuffed handfuls of sauced pasta in her mouth. I thought it was the sexiest thing on earth, and even though at the time I had adopted the affectation of eating like a European with fork in my left hand and knife in my right, to this day I prefer to eat with my hands. This dish satisfies that craving.

The large pancake is made of fermented teff flour. Some restaurants use a mixture of teff and wheat, but I think it's better made with teff alone. It's essentially a sourdough batter, left on the kitchen counter for about a week, fed with water and more teff every morning until it starts to bubble and smells pleasantly sour. If it's not quite light enough, you can always add a pinch of baking powder for extra lift.

1 C teff flour	2 Tbs spicy lime pickle
1 Tbs oil	1 jumbo egg
½ C brown lentils	

A week ahead, mix the teff with water until you have a thick batter. Every morning, add a little more water and about 1 tablespoon of teff, and mix. If in the morning you see a dark purplish water rise to the top, you can pour that off and add fresh water. At the end of that week, you're ready to move ahead.

Heat the oil to medium in a large pan, and pour in about half a cup of batter, swirling it around to cover the entire surface. You really have to eyeball this. The goal is to make a thin pancake. When you see bubbles pop through the batter, place a cover on the pan, which cooks the top. Swirl it around to make sure it's loose, and slide onto a platter. One should be enough, so feed your batter and keep it on the countertop, or use it all up.

What you put on top depends entirely on what you have in the fridge. I had cooked lentils, an Indian lime pickle, which elevated the entire dish, and then decided a fried egg would go nicely. So would a hard-boiled egg. But leftover stewed chicken would be fabulous, or even fish.

Injera

GINGER SOUFFLÉ PANCAKES

There was a long stretch of my life when I had a pancake every day for breakfast. Eventually I even wrote a little book about them, arguing that they are the food that has most dramatically influenced the course of human history. Many people didn't realize that it was satire. Can you take pancakes too seriously? I hope this recipe will convince you that pancakes are serious business, and as it really is remarkably quick and easy to prepare, I think we should permanently move pancakes from the breakfast-only category into nosherei.

    1 C pastry flour
    1 egg yolk and 1 egg white
    ⅛ tsp vanilla extract
    1 tsp baking powder
    1 tsp molasses
    1 Tbs grated ginger juice
    1 tsp powdered ginger
    ½ C buttermilk
    1 tsp sugar
    1 tsp butter
    lingonberry jam, for topping

Mix all the ingredients but the egg white and butter in a bowl with half the sugar. The ginger juice is made by grating the ginger and just squeezing out the liquid, and it keeps the pancakes light and fluffy. Add enough buttermilk to make a thick batter. In another bowl, beat the egg white until frothy, add the other half of the sugar, and keep beating until stiff. Melt the butter over high heat in a large, nonstick pan. Gently fold the egg white into the batter with a spatula and then spoon into the hot butter once it stops sizzling. You will be able to get 5 small pancakes. Lower the heat, and when you see little holes emerge in the top of the batter, turn each pancake over. Then transfer to a plate and top with a dollop of lingonberry jam. Not surprisingly, these pancakes are also excellent with savory ingredients.

SAUSAGE WAFFLES

These heart-shaped waffles remind me of the light-hearted Viennese Küsserwaf-felnwalz. Rumor has it that couples would sweep across the floor passing beneath a waffle suspended from the ceiling by a string. When the music stopped the pair beneath the waffle would kiss it twice, and only then would the music start again. To make these you really do need a proper waffle iron, made of iron, the kind that go on the stove top. For years I fiddled with electric waffle makers. They would heat erratically. The batter seeped out the sides. They were impossible to clean.

The handles fell off. I went through three before getting a real iron and then my troubles were over.

These waffles are a little unusual in that there's sausage inside. I used pre-cooked breakfast sausage. This recipe makes one large waffle with 5 heart-shaped segments. But I have also made a kind of meat waffle with raw ground sausage, and well-seasoned ground beef, lamb, or turkey. I set a patty in the waffle iron and poured the batter over and around it, and it turned out luscious. and crispy. I leave up to you the amount and type of meat to add.

½ C pastry flour
1 tsp unrefined sugar
1 Tbs buttermilk powder
1 tsp baking powder
1 jumbo egg
¼ C heavy cream
1 ½–2 Tbs water
2 breakfast links, chopped into pieces
1 Tbs butter

Mix all the ingredients except the butter. Heat the waffle iron over low heat and spread the butter all over the interior surface. Raise the heat to high and pour in the batter. Close and cook for about 1 minute, then turn over and cook the other side, also for 1 minute. Then lower the heat and continue to cook gently, checking each side periodically until it's lightly browned. Naturally, these are great with maple syrup, and maybe even a dollop of schlag, or Viennese-style whipped cream.

FISH WAFFLES

At some point, I picked up a mold used in Japan to make fish-shaped cakes called *taiyaki*. The Japanese take these very seriously, and they are seriously sweet, too, filled with bean paste, or sometimes chocolate or custard. I could never manage to finish one. So why not make them savory? And flavor them with actual fish? That resolves the cognitive dissonance of eating a sweet pastry fish.

½ C pastry flour
1 tsp baking powder
2 Tbs buttermilk powder
1 tsp instant dashi powder
1 jumbo egg
¼ C dry sake
4 oz raw tuna cut into small cubes
1 Tbs butter

Mix all the ingredients, except the butter. Heat the fish mold gently and spread with butter. Then turn the burner up to high. Carefully pour in the batter and close the lid, cooking on high heat for a minute. Turn over and cook the other side. Then lower the heat and continue cooking each side, checking now and then until they are nicely browned, about 5 minutes. These really want to be served with Bull-Dog Tonkatsu Sauce and Kewpie mayonnaise.

Fish Waffles

FRUITCAKE

Fruitcake simply gets a bad rap. I don't know whether it's because there's so much bad fruitcake out there made with second-rate ingredients, or whether people resent being given cake as a holiday gift and find it funny to pass it along to others year after year. I insist that it is the one cake that should be taken absolutely seriously. First, there's the riot of intense dried fruit, the powerful punch of spices, including pepper, and most important, the booze. It's a grown-up cake if ever there was one. This version is expensive because there's so much in it, but it is extremely easy to make and makes a superb nosh, especially with a slice of Wensleydale, sharp cheddar, or double Gloucester on the side. And remember, never frost a fruit cake.

The proportions of ingredients are up to you. Here they were dictated by the size of the packages available. The recipe makes two 9″ × 5″ rectangular cakes. Give one away as a holiday gift, and keep the other for yourself.

6 oz prunes
5 oz dried cherries
10 oz dates
6 oz apricots
1 C dried white mulberries
6 oz raisins
1 C crystallized ginger
4 strips candied orange peel
2 C walnut pieces
3 C merlot or other red wine
2 C sugar
1 tsp salt
½ freshly grated nutmeg
1 Tbs freshly ground cinnamon
1 Tbs freshly ground black pepper
¼ C dark molasses
5 jumbo eggs
2 Tbs baking powder
2 Tbs buttermilk powder
2 sticks melted butter (16 Tbsp or ½ lb)
3 C cake flour
1 C dark rum

Chop all the fruit (except for the cherries and raisins) into small pieces. Leave the cherries and raisins whole. Add the ginger, candied orange peel, and walnuts, and pour the wine over the mixture. Stir, and let it soak in about 10 minutes, stirring from time to time. Add all the other ingredients in order and mix thoroughly. Just be sure your butter isn't too hot when you add it or you'll cook the eggs. Then butter your baking tins, pour in the mixture, and bake in a preheated oven at 350°F for 1 hour. Remove, let cool for a few hours, and pour over about ¼ cup of rum. The next day, add more rum. Continue adding a splash of rum every day until you are ready to eat the cake, or until you think it's boozy enough. Contrary to what people say, you don't have to make this months before the holidays. A few days of boozing up the cake are fine. And, yes, let me remind you, this is for noshing, not dessert.

PEA SOUP PANCAKE AND MUFFIN

Dense and smoky pea soup is so satisfying on a cold day that I couldn't resist turning it into a snack food one chilly morning. These are surprisingly light and fluffy and crisp on the edges, and much more interesting than a regular wheat flour pancake.

½ C green split peas
½ C milk
½ tsp salt
2 slices bacon
1 small shallot, finely sliced
1 tsp baking powder
¼ tsp lemon juice
Maple syrup or okonomiyaki/BBQ sauce

Cover the split peas with water and soak overnight. Drain and rinse them well in a fine-meshed sieve. Put them in a blender with the milk and salt. Process until a smooth batter. Set aside.

Slice the bacon into small lardons and fry gently in a cast-iron skillet, rendering the fat completely. Remove the bacon and set aside. Cook the shallot slices in the fat, and set that aside, and keep the bacon grease hot. Once the bacon and shallot are cool, mix into the batter, add the baking powder and lemon juice. Stir well. Pour half the batter into the hot fat and let cook until bubbles appear on the surface. Lower the heat and cook on the other side, sliding a thin metal spatula underneath from time to time so that it doesn't stick. Repeat with the rest of the batter. Serve the pancakes with syrup or sauce.

This same batter also makes an excellent muffin. If you combine the same soaked peas, milk, salt, and baking powder, but also add a tablespoon of buttermilk powder and a teaspoon of sugar, they can be baked in a muffin tin. Use liquid buttermilk instead of the milk, if that's what you have on hand. Bake at 450°F for 15 minutes. Makes 6 small muffins. I ate them with a tahini and yogurt sauce, some chopped basil, and a few slices of avocado with lime juice. Splendid. Another variation follows immediately.

Pea Soup Pancake and Muffin

HAM AND SPLIT PEA PIKELETS WITH APPLE BUTTER

Despite what the name might suggest, these are not little fish; rather, "pikelet" is a charming term the Scots use for pancakes about the size of a silver dollar. The surprising twist is the base, made entirely from dried peas. The flavor profile of the final dish replicates the familiar soup, too. If you have a powerful food processor or Vitamix machine, there's no need to soak the peas, but doing so does make the final pancake a little lighter and fluffier. This recipe should take about 10 minutes and makes 10 little pancakes, or servings for 2 or 3 people. Simply double for a larger group.

1 C dried green split peas
1 C whole milk
1 jumbo egg
1 tsp salt
2 tsp baking powder
1 Tbs malted milk powder
2 Tbs buttermilk powder
1 tsp dried sage
¼ tsp ground black pepper
¼ tsp cayenne pepper
¼ tsp smoked paprika
¼ tsp garlic powder
⅛ tsp Madras curry powder
One slice or 6.5 oz Smithfield ham, diced
2 Tbs lard or peanut oil

Garnish: apple butter and red currants

Soak the peas overnight in water, rinse, and drain thoroughly. In a blender, add the peas, milk, and egg, and process for about 1 minute until completely smooth. Transfer to a mixing bowl and add all the dry ingredients, spices, and the ham in very fine dice. Mix thoroughly. Heat the fat to medium in a large skillet and drop the batter in by the spoonful. When holes begin to appear on top, flip the pancakes over with a spatula and cook until both sides are lightly brown. Transfer to a rack and continue with a second batch. To serve, put a little apple butter on the side and a little sour fruit such as fresh red currants.

If you are inclined to make your own apple butter, simply cut 6 apples into large pieces, cover with water, add 2 Tbs sugar. Simmer for 1 hour, then pass through a food mill. Then cook that sauce another hour or longer over very low heat until brown and thick. Makes one pint jar.

Ham and Split Pea Pikelets with Apple Butter

HOT WATER CORN BREAD

When I was young, my parents sent me to summer camp in the Pocono mountains of northeast Pennsylvania. This meant sleeping in a big canvas tent surrounded by trees. I got so used to being immersed in nature for two months a year that it still feels wrong staying home for the summer. Whether we were intentionally taught or simply absorbed the wisdom of the forest, it became a regular supply of food. There was birch bark and sassafras root to make tea, blueberries fermented into a coarse wine, and abundant perch in the lake. One summer my tent was right at water's edge, and I could cast a line from my bed. On "cookout" nights when we were expected to make hamburgers, it was a chance to cook anything wild. I became so enthralled by cooking over flames that my parents let me dig a firepit in the backyard, and I used to make soup from wild onions and once baked a pie outside with our sour cherries.

To this day I can vouch for the gastronomic superiority of food cooked over an open flame. Smoke is a primal flavor, hard-wired into our senses over countless generations of sitting around a campfire, telling stories, dancing, and being mesmerized by the flames. Cooking in a fireplace comes close but is somehow too comfortable. You have to be caked with dirt, sore from gathering firewood, or aching after a strenuous hike. Food simply tastes better generated by this type of hunger. I can vividly recall nearly every meal I've cooked over a fire, including the failures. There were beans that refused to soften in the altitude of the Sierras and a sack of potatoes hauled up Mount Washington, never to be eaten because the sun suddenly set. But on one camping trip we were given fresh abalone, pounded with a hammer, breaded with cracker crumbs, and gently fried in butter. Or a whole pig skewered on a pole and slowly roasted over glowing embers.

The culinary pleasures of campfire cooking extend to noshing, too: cowboy coffee boiled in a blue enamel pot, pancakes and bacon sizzling in a cast-iron skillet. And the colder it is early in the morning, the better the food tastes. If you can't see your breath, it's not quite so satisfying. So if you find yourself in the mountains with a roaring fire early in the morning, this kind of hot water cornbread is perfect, especially eaten with dirty fingers. The idea of measuring ingredients is absurd in this context.

> Bacon (or dry salami if you're hiking)
> Cornmeal
> Salt
> Boiling water

Prop three rocks around a small pile of burning twigs and branches. Place a cast-iron skillet on top and fry the bacon in it. To the side, have a pot of water nestled in the embers, brought to the boil. When the bacon is done, remove it from the pan and set aside. Pour some of the boiling water into the cornmeal with a little salt, until it makes a thick batter. Put a tea bag in the pot to steep in the rest of the water. Drop spoonfuls of the batter into the sizzling bacon grease. When brown on one side, cook on the other. If you're cooking for many people, you may need to do many batches with added bacon grease. If you happen to have foraged some wild greens, such as dandelion, miner's lettuce, or wood sorrel (sour clover), wilt it in the pan at the end. It complements the corn bread and bacon perfectly.

CHICKEN AND RICE FRITTERS

You should always make more rice than you need, simply because it is the best ingredient to turn into something completely different. Here I was thinking of calas—the sweet rice fritters of New Orleans—but couldn't get Italian supplì with chicken out of my mind. This recipe is savory but still somewhere between the two. Likewise, this recipe straddles the fine line between the sublime and the ridiculous. It makes about 14 small, round fritters. Of course, double the recipe if you have more people or are averse to using half an egg.

½ C leftover cooked basmati rice
¼ C cooked chicken breast, finely shredded
¼ C green bell pepper, diced
¼ tsp candied orange peel, chopped
¼ tsp almond extract
¼ C pastry flour
½ tsp baking powder
½ Tbs chicken fat
½ egg
¼ tsp salt, plus more for sprinkling
24 oz peanut oil

Gently break up the cold rice with your fingers so that all the grains are separate. Add every ingredient thereafter, the chicken, pepper, peel, and so forth, stirring and making sure there are no clumps as you go. The egg alone will bind everything into a light batter. Heat your oil over a medium flame. Using a ⅜ inch scoop, drop little balls into the hot fat and let them fry, just a few minutes until golden brown, and drain on paper towels. Sprinkle with extra salt if you like.

Serve these with a dip of your choice. I used equal parts mayo, ketchup, and sriracha, which is a standard at my house. You can also use chimichurri made of cilantro, parsley, olive oil, and vinegar. If you are feeling really deranged, sprinkle with powdered sugar. The flavor combination is very medieval and quite charming.

FLUFFY COTTAGE CHEESE PANCAKES

Many years ago I was at the Oxford Symposium chatting with my old friend Andy Smith about editing food encyclopedias and book series, something both of us were usually up to our necks in. He said that he had an idea to do a series of little books, each of which would focus on a single food or ingredient and, off the cuff, asked if I wanted to do one. Without even thinking, I said, Sure, how about pancakes? Done. I figured that, as I had spent many years in graduate school making pancakes every morning from every type of flour I could find, it would be a breeze. And in fact, it was—but here's one recipe that I regretfully never managed to include in that book.

> 1 egg white
> 1 tsp sugar
> ½ C white pastry flour
> 1 tsp baking powder
> ⅛ tsp salt
> ⅓ C cottage cheese
> ½ C whole milk
> ⅛ tsp vanilla extract
> 1 Tbs butter

Whip the egg white until light and frothy, add the sugar, and continue beating until fairly stiff. In another bowl, sift the flour, baking powder, and salt. Add the cottage cheese, milk, and vanilla, and stir thoroughly. Heat the butter in a large skillet. Gently fold the egg whites into the batter with a rubber spatula. Drop three globs of batter into the sizzling butter and lower the heat. After a few minutes, turn them over, and continue cooking until nicely browned on both sides. Place the three little pancakes on a plate and spoon over some of your favorite jam. I used black currant.

MULTIGRAIN DOSA WITH CHOUCROUTE

A traditional dosa takes a deft hand, but with a little practice, it's not too difficult. This, of course, is not a traditional dosa, but something more like a big, naturally fermented crepe, but aesthetically it's similar. You can make 3 large crepes with this batter or many smaller ones.

> 3 Tbs each: urad dal, basmati rice, dried chickpeas, millet, amaranth, corn grits
> 1 Tbs green lentils
> Heel of stale sourdough bread

Cover everything with water and let sit one day in a bowl covered with a cloth to start fermenting. Then liquefy in a Vitamix or other blender and let sit for another day. Over a medium flame, heat a little oil or butter on a nonstick pan or a traditional tawa. Thin out the batter until it can be poured. Take one ladleful and pour it in the middle of the pan and swirl it around with the bottom of the ladle until it covers most of the pan. Cook for about 2 minutes until you can release it and there are holes on top. Flip over and cook the other side. Then remove to a plate.

You can wrap virtually anything in these. I happened to have been slow-cooking a pint of sauerkraut with 3 slices of bacon chopped finely, white sausages, a pig's foot, onion, and caraway, plus a cup of wine. You just throw it all in a pot and simmer on the lowest heat for hours. It complements the dosa so nicely.

Muffins, Biscuits, and Scones

FOUR SAVORY MUFFINS

After my father retired, he took up muffin making with a fury that reflected his interest not in cooking, per se, but in eating baked goods. He used to perform a trick I saw on many occasions. We would park the car somewhere we had never been. Dad would hop out of the car and put his nose in the air and immediately follow the scent down the street. Without fail, he would find the local bakery. This was true and honest talent; we had not passed the bakery in the car, nor was there any way to search it on a phone back then. When we arrived, he would buy one of everything, break open each item and taste, throwing the vast majority away: "this is garbage"; "too sweet"; "greasy." Maybe one or two items would meet with his approval, and if we were lucky, the rest of the family would get to taste, too.

I mention all this because I think it's why I have never made muffins. It was his terrain, and in homage I never tried to replicate his muffins, and honestly I never liked muffins much, certainly not the massive wads of sweet, oily dough available in most markets. My father's were very good—whole wheat, laden with carrots or other vegetables, walnuts, oil rather than butter, not too sweet. He practiced a lot. I have not. I threw everything in bowls and hoped it would work. They all did.

This will take a little time, so ideally it is something you do ahead and enjoy through the week. It's also pointless to make one small batch, because all the time is in baking them. So I give you recipes for 12 small (2 ½ inch) muffins, all including ingredients I love. First the master batter, then the fillings.

Batter
2 C pastry flour
1 Tbs baking powder
1 Tbs unrefined sugar
½ tsp salt
½ stick butter (4 Tbsp), melted but not hot
½ C yogurt
½ C milk
1 large egg

In a large bowl, add the dry ingredients and whisk together. Then mix the wet ingredients together in another bowl. Set these aside until you are ready to bake.

Filling No. 1: Dice 2 tablespoons of pancetta and lightly cook until no longer raw. Shred a string cheese–worth of mozzarella,(a scant handful) chop a few tablespoons of parsley, and splash with 1 tablespoon of limoncello. Place in a bowl.

Filling No. 2: Cut up 2 sticks of surimi, and add a few pieces of purple pickled Japanese eggplant (shibazuke), 1 tablespoon of finely diced fresh ginger, and 1 tablespoon of dry sake. Place in a bowl.

Filling No. 3: Shred 1 slice of supermarket roasted cold cut turkey, 5 cremini mushrooms sliced and sautéed in butter, 2 tablespoons of shredded aged Gouda, and 1 tablespoon of pinot grigio wine. Place in a bowl.

Filling No. 4: Chop 1 jalapeño, 1 scallion, a few sprigs of cilantro, some crumbled cotija cheese, juice of one-quarter of a lime, and 1 tablespoon of tequila. Place in a bowl.

Now preheat your oven to 400°F. Arrange 12 small, paper-lined muffin cups in a metal baking pan. Add the wet ingredients to the dry to make the batter, just stirring until they come together. Then divide that equally among each of the 4 bowls containing the other ingredients. It should be a lumpy, slightly dense batter. If you need to add a little more liquid, add a little more of the alcohol you already used in each bowl.

Apportion the contents of each bowl into the muffin cups. Each should fill 3, so you will have 12 muffins in all. Place in the oven and bake for 15 minutes. Let cool, then enjoy.

CORN MUFFINS

The best corn muffins I've ever tasted were sold in the basement under the School of Architecture, at Columbia University. I went to grad school there, in the History Department. I never bought anything else from this little pop-up stand. The muffins were explosively corn-flavored, and I've never been able to replicate that taste. Nor did the muffins need any adornment. These too are awfully good plain, especially if you can find excellent cornmeal. If that means paying a lot for it online, I think the difference is palpable. And when gussied up as they are here, well, fantastic.

1 ⅓ C cornmeal	¼ C melted butter
⅔ C pastry flour	1 Tbs dark honey
2 tsp baking powder	Pinch of mace
½ tsp salt	2 slices thick-cut bacon
1 egg	1 Tbs green pepper jelly
1 C buttermilk	Pinch of za'atar

Mix everything together and pour into 8 greased muffin tins, or 6 if you like them larger with a big top. Bake 20 minutes at 400°F. Chop the bacon into matchstick or lardon shapes, and fry gently so the fat is rendered. Remove the bacon to a paper towel to drain. When cooked and cooled slightly, cut the muffins horizontally and fry in the remaining bacon grease, face down, until crispy and browned. Add a dollop of the jelly, then the bacon, and a sprinkling of zaʾatar.

Corn Muffins

PROPER BISCUITS

These are some proper biscuits, light flaky and rising elegantly layer upon layer. If you can get White Lily flour, it is preferred throughout the South. But I have found unbleached pastry flour, low in gluten, to be excellent, too. Years ago my friend Kimmy and I made biscuits with Saw Mill gravy—basically, just sausages, flour, and milk. It's great, but only if you're fixing to saw down trees all day. I tried a few different combinations for fillings, all of which were very good. But maybe a slice of country ham is really the best option.

1 ¼ C unbleached pastry flour, plus more for dusting
1 Tbs baking powder
½ tsp sugar
⅓ tsp sea salt
4 Tbs salted Irish butter
½ C buttermilk
¼ tsp rice wine vinegar

Preheat your oven to 425°F. In a large bowl, mix the first four dry ingredients, then cut in the butter with a pastry cutter until you have many little lumps. Pour in the buttermilk, and mix just until it all comes together. I added the dash of vinegar to bring it all into a solid mass and give it a little bite. Place on a wooden board dusted with flour and roll out. Fold into quarters and roll out again. Do this four more times. Then, using a round pastry cutter, plunge directly down into the dough, without twisting, so you have four circles. Bake for 15 minutes with the scraps on the side as a treat for the baker. Or roll into another biscuit if you like.

One fetching combination I added to these was a large shiitake mushroom fried, a circle of red bell pepper the same size as the biscuit, also fried, and some corn relish. If you ever have a mind to make your own corn relish, just cut the corn off the cob. Sauté in a pan with olive oil, 1 shallot, some red bell pepper, a quarter-cup of vinegar, and a quarter-cup of sugar. Add 1 teaspoon of salt and one-quarter teaspoon of turmeric. Let it cook down until thick and then put in a jar in the fridge. It will last a few weeks there.

This here biscuit was also superb with a small patty of turkey sausage and some cheese sauce poured over. The latter I made with about half a cup of sauvignon blanc wine, a pinch of sodium citrate, and some leftover bits of cheese, heated in a pan. It came out a tad lumpy but still really good. I poured it over the sausage and sprinkled with tarragon.

Believe it or not, the biscuit was also excellent with some soft, finely shredded, dried and smoked squid, kelp gossamer, katsuobushi flakes, and togarashi powder. All these can be found at a Japanese grocery store, and the net effect is not unlike the smoky country ham.

Proper Biscuits

CREAM BISCUITS

I'm not sure why I thought biscuits were the sort of thing you needed years of practice, and a real southern background, to make properly. At least, this very simple version took neither of these. Naturally, sausage gravy or a slice of country ham would be ideal with these biscuits, but I think any sort of leftovers also work wonderfully. Just for kicks I tried it with tomato and mozzarella, too, and it was great. But so was the smoky baba ghanoush.

1 C pastry flour or all-purpose flour	½ tsp salt
1 tsp sugar	¾ C heavy cream
½ tsp baking powder	

Preheat the oven to 425°F. Mix the dry ingredients. Add the cream, and stir just until it comes together. Gently divide into three small handfuls and place them on a baking sheet lined with parchment paper. Bake 15 minutes, then let cool. They should look rough, and all the nubbly bits will have browned nicely.

With Baba Ghanoush

1 eggplant	1 tsp za'atar
1 Tbs tahini	1 Tbs lemon juice
1 tsp salt	

Place the eggplant directly over a gas flame and char on all sides. You can do this on the barbecue, too. Alternatively, I've also peeled, sliced, and microwaved the eggplant in a casserole. You won't get the smoky flavor, but it's still good. For the charred version, scrape out the flesh, add all the other ingredients to it, and mash thoroughly.

Place the baba ghanoush on your split biscuit with some sautéed broccoli rabe, a little crumbled feta, or whatever you have on hand.

Other very interesting things I've put on these biscuits include sausage and baked beans, leftover fried chicken slices with hot sauce, and even sweet bean paste to replicate a steamed bun.

COCONUT BISCUITS WITH PERSIMMON AND CASHEW DUKKAH

To my surprise, the very simple cream biscuit, or drop biscuit as they're called, also works wonderfully with coconut cream. This is the solid layer that forms at the top of a can of coconut milk. Don't use coconut oil; that will not work here.

1 C pastry or all-purpose flour
1 tsp baking powder
1 tsp sugar
½ tsp salt
½ C coconut cream
½ extravagantly overripe hachiya persimmon almost at the point of
    disintegration
¼ C crushed cashews seasoned with salt, cumin, coriander, cayenne
    pepper

Mix the first four dry ingredients and moisten with the coconut cream. You want a dough that holds together, but just barely. You may need to add a little more liquid, but don't overmix. Just form into a circle and drop on a baking sheet and bake for about 15 minutes until brown. Let cool and then fill with the persimmon, just spooned on, and sprinkle with the dukkah. Put the top on and enjoy.

FRIED OYSTERS ON BANNOCKS

If you live inland you will understand the deep yearning for salty spray, the sound of cackling gulls, the ineffably pungent aroma of the sea that leaves you craving oysters or crab. When I get to the ocean, the first thing I do is run up to the tide where it breaks upon the sand, scoop up some water, and anoint my head with the brine. I actually live in a seaport, 90 miles inland, but it is as far from the sea emotionally as one can get, mostly because we rarely find great seafood in the market. And we're a few hours from the beach. So imagine my delight one day when six different types of live oysters suddenly appeared in my grocery with no explanation. I bought some Fanny Bay oysters and this is what they inspired.

Bannocks or farls
1 C oat flour
2 Tbs butter, with a little reserved for greasing the skillet
1 tsp salt
1 tsp baking powder
½ C buttermilk
Splash whiskey or other booze

Mix all the ingredients well. Don't worry about overmixing; it won't become tough. You can form into one large bannock, divide into 4 quarters as farls, or just mold 4 little rounded circles with your hands. Place the dough in a greased skillet (or "girdle," as they say in Scotland) on low heat. Cook gently for 10 minutes each side. You can also bake them in a slow oven. Then proceed to the next steps:

Opulent Nosh

2 round oat bannocks
4 oysters
1 egg
½ C fine bread crumbs
1 Tbs butter
Japanese seaweed paste (tsukudani)
broccoli microgreens or other tiny sprout

If you have thick farls, split them. Thin, round bannocks will work fine on their own. Dip the oysters in beaten egg, then into bread crumbs. Place in a pan with hot butter, then lay on a paper towel to drain. Spread the paste on the bannocks and place 2 oysters on each. Garnish with the sprouts.

Fried Oysters on Bannocks

SCONES

This is for my British and Australian friends who look at American biscuits and call them "scones." These aren't scones in the proper Scots sense of lumps of oaten dough cooked on a "girdle," that is, griddle. But nothing that people make nowadays are biscuits either. The very name "bis-cuit" means "twice baked." Only biscotti are exactly that, and I guess ship's biscuit, if anyone still makes those. But these are cousins of southern biscuits, just gussied up with fillings that border on the savory. Adding savory ingredients in the middle after baking gives you opulent sandwiches.

1 ¼ C unbleached pastry flour
¼ C coarse raw sugar, plus 1 Tbs for sprinkling over after baking
⅓ tsp fine sea salt
½ Tbs baking powder
4 Tbs unsalted butter
½ C fresh cranberries
½ C mixed nuts (almonds, pecans, hazelnuts, cashews), chopped
½ inch sprig of fresh rosemary
1 jumbo egg
1 tsp almond extract
½ C whole cream

Preheat the oven to 425°F. I use my toaster oven so I don't heat the whole house up. In a large mixing bowl, combine the flour, sugar, and baking powder, then cut in the cold butter until there are small nubbins of butter evenly distributed. Add the cranberries. Add the coarsely chopped nuts. Then strip the rosemary off the stem, chop finely, and add that. In another bowl, mix the egg, extract, and cream. Mix the contents of the two bowls quickly, just until it all comes together into a shaggy mass. Plop it onto a floured board and flatten into a circle with your floured hands. Cut into quarters and place the wedges on a parchment-lined baking sheet. Bake for 23 minutes until brown and the cranberries have begun to ooze. Sprinkle on the extra sugar. Let cool.

Slice a scone horizontally and fill with turkey and cheese—or be creative with fillings. I tried ham, and unsurprisingly it was fabulous. If you're really daring, duck liver pâté is also unfathomably delectable.

MEDITERRANEAN SCONES

Most store-bought scones are just not that thrilling. They're sort of dry and chalky, and way too sweet. A savory iteration solves both those problems, and despite the bold flavors in these, they will go with practically anything inside, including clotted cream.

1 C white pastry flour

1 tsp baking powder

½ tsp salt

2 tsp unrefined sugar, plus
    extra for sprinkling

½ C sun-dried tomatoes

¼ C pine nuts

1 tsp crumbled dry sage

1 tsp crumbled dry oregano

¼ C cold salted butter

5 Tbs evaporated milk

1 egg

1 tsp fig balsamic vinegar

Preheat the oven to 400°F. Mix all the dry ingredients, add in the butter, and work into crumbly bits with your fingers. Add the wet ingredients, but only half the egg, and stir just until it all comes together. Divide into 4 parts, place them on a parchment-lined baking sheet, and flatten into disks. Brush on the remaining egg and sprinkle lightly with some sugar. Bake immediately for 20 minutes. Remove and let cook completely on a rack.

Now the real question is what to put on these. My thoughts immediately go to fish. A few sardines or oily mackerel would be ideal. But tuna or a lighter fish would be nice. So too would a sausage patty, or some leftover chicken.

Mediterranean Scones

Fritters

SALT COD WITH ROMESCO AND ESCAROLE

Fritters
1 lb box bacalao (salt cod)
2 Tbs olive oil
¼ C heavy cream
½ C dry fino sherry
1 C okonomiyaki flour or regular pancake mix, plus more if necessary for a
      very thick batter
1 Tbs lard or butter

Romesco Sauce
2 large red peppers
½ C toasted almonds, crushed
2 cloves garlic
¼ C olive oil
1 tsp salt

Escarole
1 head of escarole
2 Tbs olive oil
Salt to taste

Dabs of mayonnaise
1 small hot red chili pepper, thinly sliced

Soak the bacalao in water for 24 hours in the fridge, changing the water often. Sauté it gently in olive oil until it begins to fall apart, then transfer to a bowl. Add the cream and the sherry, and mix until the fish has broken up completely. Then add the okonomiyaki flour. With your hands, roll the batter into a dozen small balls and fry in a pan with hemispherical depressions such as an æbleskiver or takoyaki pan, or simply fry in a regular nonstick pan. Fry until golden brown and then transfer to a rack to cool.

For the romesco sauce, place the red peppers directly on the gas burner or grill, and turn frequently until completely charred. Place in a large paper bag until cool. Scrape off the char with a knife (do not rinse), remove the seeds and core, and chop the pepper finely. Place in a pan with the garlic and olive oil and cook gently until soft. Add salt. Then transfer to a mortar and pound until it becomes a chunky sauce. Lastly, add the almonds.

Chop the escarole and sauté in the oil until tender. Add salt to taste while cooking.

To serve, arrange the fritters on a plate with the sauce and the escarole on the side. Garnish with the mayonnaise and slivers of chili pepper.

Salt Cod with Romesco and Escarole

IN PRAISE OF POTATOES (FRIED, HASH BROWNS, SCALLOPED)

No one doubts that potatoes are among the most perfect of foods. Nevertheless, too often they are treated with abuse and neglect. We have all had soggy, greasy hash browns and french fries that have lost their crunch. I offer here three techniques that are simple and quick, and can easily be used whenever you're feeling peckish. For the first one, you will have to purge yourself of any prejudice you may harbor against the microwave oven. I grew up with an intense fear of microwave ovens and believed they were the work of the devil. I now use mine almost daily, not only to defrost food, but also to cook certain vegetables, especially eggplants, zucchini, and potatoes, all of which contain an abundance of water. These recipes are intended specifically for the Russet Burbank but would probably work with any potato variety.

FRIED POTATOES

Take one potato. Put it in the microwave for 7 minutes. If you make two, then let it go for about 11; for three about 15. This depends entirely on the size of the potato and your particular machine, so better to undercook and then have to put it in for another minute or so. The potato is done when it no longer feels hard inside. Slice it in half lengthwise. Then slice into quarters. Then either cook these as wedges or chop into smaller pieces, as you please. Heat a few tablespoons of oil on low in a nonstick skillet. Salt your potatoes and then add the microwaved pieces into the pan. Turn them over now and then, and continue frying gently until brown and crispy. Drain on a paper towel and serve. Now just think of how much easier this is than deep-frying, and how much crisper they are on the outside and soft on the inside than regular fried potatoes. If you are in the mood, fry some chopped onions and peppers in the same pan and toss them together with the potatoes at the last minute—but not sooner, to keep the potatoes from losing their crunch.

HASH BROWNS OR LATKES

Peel one potato and shred it into a large bowl using the large holes of a grater. Squeeze out all the water into another bowl. You will be surprised by how much of a potato is water. Let that rest for a few minutes and discard the water. At the bottom of the bowl you'll see starch that has settled; add that back to the potatoes. Heat about ¼ inch of peanut oil in a nonstick skillet. Make 4 balls of the potato and place them in the oil. Flatten them with a spatula and fry until golden brown. Turn over and fry the other side. When perfectly crispy, remove them and let them drain on paper towels, then transfer to a plate. They stay wonderfully crisp. Excellent noshing!

I like to use these as a vehicle for other foods. Sour cream is great, especially topped with caviar. A crumble of feta cheese and chopped olives is great. Just be sure not to add anything watery, or they will go soft. A little bacon, lime pickle, and cheese is magnificent. Or just eat them as is, ungarnished.

SCALLOPED POTATOES

This is the easiest technique. Peel the potato, slice it into thin rounds, and put the rounds in a small ramekin, salting each layer as you go. You can add chives or onions if you wish. Then dump in heavy cream so everything is barely covered. It will take about half a cup. Put it in the microwave for about 7 minutes or slightly longer, when the top begins to brown. That's all. You can also make a big casserole and cook it in the oven if you prefer, but this is a quick nosh. I turn out the whole thing on a plate, top with a fried egg maybe and a dash of Tajín seasoning. Or a little furikake.

PORK PIE POT STICKER

The seasonings and texture of this quick dumpling lean more toward Britain than China, hence the name. You might think this takes a lot of time and skill, but it doesn't, and you're really only making two big ravioli. The time it will take you to roll out the dough is about 5 minutes, and the results more than make up for the effort expended. The balance of seasonings is only a suggestion; I never measure them.

¼ lb ground pork	½ C flour
1 tsp salt	¼ C water or less
¼ tsp pepper	Pinch of salt
¼ tsp thyme	1 egg
⅛ tsp mace	2 Tbs olive oil
⅛ tsp mustard powder	Hot water

Mix the pork and seasonings well. I often like to chop pork shoulder myself with a cleaver to get a smooth texture, but ground pork is fine. Mix the flour, salt, and just enough water so that it comes together as a dough, probably less than a quarter-cup. Knead until incorporated and then divide into 4 small balls. Roll each of these out into a circle. Put half the pork mixture on two of the circles. Beat the egg in a small bowl and brush the other two circles, then affix them on top, pressing out any air pockets. If you want to trim these to get a neat edge, use a glass to cut them. You can even crimp the edges, as I have done. Heat the olive oil in a nonstick pan and fry the little pies on low heat until just beginning to brown. Then turn the heat up to high and pour in hot water until they're just covered. Flip them over. When the water has evaporated, the pot stickers are done. Serve with HP Sauce on the side or A.1. if you can't find that. Barbecue sauce is good, too.

TUNA CHURROS WITH PASILLA DIPPING SAUCE

These are light and fluffy on the inside and crunchy on the outside, although still weirdly reminiscent of a tuna sandwich. The dipping sauce is very spicy, so you won't need a lot.

Churros

3 oz white albacore tuna in water, drained	⅓ C buttermilk
1 Tbs mayonnaise	½ tsp tarragon
½ tsp baking powder	½ qt frying oil, around 2 inches deep
⅓ C pastry flour	

Sauce

1 pasilla negro chili	½ tsp salt
1 C boiling water	1 tsp oil
1 small shallot	

Start by cracking the chili and removing most of the seeds, then pour the boiling water over and let soak about 10 minutes. In an electric blender, mix the chili with the shallot and salt, and pulverize until smooth. Then fry this liquid in a shallow pan in hot oil. Let it reduce gently until you have a thick sauce and put in a small bowl. (You'll probably have plenty left over for enchiladas.)

Then mix the batter using all the aforementioned ingredients, except the oil. Heat up the oil over a medium flame. With a rubber spatula, scrape the batter into a piping bag fitted with a star tip. Then squeeze out lines into the hot oil. You'll have to do this in two batches, but they only take 2–3 minutes or so to cook. When golden brown, let them drain on a paper towel. Sprinkle with salt if you like. Serve with the dipping sauce.

A SUITE OF CHICKPEAS

Can you think of a more remarkably versatile ingredient than the adorable little chickpea? Everyone loves hummus with tahini. Falafel in pita bread is miraculous. Then there's *farinata* and its cousin *socca,* crunchy baked chickpea and olive oil flatbread, best made in a wood-burning oven. Or a thick Spanish *potaje de garbanzos,* as well as the countless fried snacks based on besan, or chickpea flour, in India. We go through at least one big can of chickpeas every week in my house, and they are one of the few things that taste good right from the can. And don't forget that the water, or aquafaba, can sub in for egg white.

For these recipes, I suggest using either dried chickpeas or chickpea flour. Canned or precooked chickpeas won't work. Like all beans, if you buy them from a store that serves people who typically eat a lot of dried beans, then they will probably be fresh. In the United States, that generally means an Indian, Latino, or Mediterranean store. At a regular supermarket, the beans may have been sitting on the shelf for ages.

Chickpea Pancakes with Tuna, Capers, and Olives

½ C chickpea flour
½ tsp baking powder
1 tsp buttermilk powder
Water
3 Tbs olive oil

1 small (3 oz) can tuna, drained
1 Tbs mayonnaise
1 Tbs capers
6 Niçoise olives, pitted

Mix the first three dry ingredients and add water until you have a thin, pourable batter. Heat the olive oil in a large (12 inch) nonstick frying pan over high heat. Pour in the batter and swirl it around so it evenly coats the entire surface. Then lower the heat to medium-low and, when bubbles begin to appear on the surface, flip the pancake with a large spatula. Cook on the other side and, when lightly browned, transfer to a plate. Then mix the other ingredients, spread the mixture in the pancake, and roll it up.

Chickpea Æbleskiver

1 C dried chickpeas
1 tsp baking powder
1 tsp buttermilk powder
1 tsp salt

¼ C fresh parsley, chopped
⅛ tsp each pepper, paprika, garlic powder
2 Tbs vegetable oil

This is not really an æbleskiver, but because I made them in a pan made for that purpose, it seems like the best name. Soak the chickpeas for 24 hours barely covered in water. Then grind the chickpeas and the soaking water in a blender or food processor on high speed for about 1 minute, until very smooth. Add the other dry ingredients, parsley, and spices. It should be a very thick batter. Heat up your æbleskiver pan with a bit of oil in each depression. (Any pan with hemispherical holes, such as a Japanese takoyaki pan, will work for this purpose.) Scoop the batter into the holes and cook over medium heat. After a couple of minutes, turn them over with a sharp skewer. The trick is to catch the very edge with the point of the skewer and flip it over without crushing the dough. Then turn again after a few minutes to brown all sides. They will form neat little balls, not crunchy like falafel, but much easier to make. Serve with a tahini sauce made of equal parts sesame paste and yogurt.

Chickpea Æbleskiver

Chickpea Idli

These use the same batter as the preceding recipe, but they are steamed. For steaming, I used a metal egg-poaching device that I found at the back of a cabinet. I have no idea how it got there and I'd never seen it before. But it is very much like a traditional Indian chickpea steamer and makes delicate little poufy rounds of chickpea. The texture was so evanescent that it seemed like a well-formed matzo ball, and indeed it went beautifully in chicken soup with carrots. If making it specifically for that purpose, substitute dill for the parsley.

Chickpea or Fava Bean Blini

Incidentally, you can use fava beans in all the chickpea recipes above, too. I've never seen fava bean flour, but I made it myself with dry blanched and shelled beans whizzed in an industrial spice grinder. There is one thing that you should not do with fava beans though: ferment the batter. It smells horrid.

> ½ C chickpea or fava bean flour
> ½ tsp baking powder
> 1 tsp buttermilk powder
> Water
> 1 Tbs butter
> 1 whole kumquat, grated
> 2 Tbs sour cream
> 2 Tbs black lumpfish caviar

Mix the dry ingredients, and add water until you have a thick pancake batter. Heat the butter in a large, nonstick skillet and drop in small spoonfuls of the batter. Lower the heat and cook until brown on one side, then turn over. Transfer to a plate. Sprinkle with the kumquat, add a dollop of the sour cream to each, and then top with some caviar. This goes perfectly with champagne.

SEV NACHOS

Among the most ingenious ways to transform chickpea flour is to extrude it through a cranked brass device used in India to make sev, a kind of fried noodle that goes into a variety of dishes. There are various other machines that will work just as well, such as a small, hand-held noodle extruder, a ricer, or even a cookie press with a perforated die. Friends testing this recipe in an online session even had success with a colander, pushing the batter through the holes, and with a cheese grater. Here, I have obviously desecrated a revered snack food, but it is so remarkably delicious, I implore you to try it.

    1 C chickpea flour
    1 tsp vegetable oil
    ½ tsp salt
    ½ tsp turmeric
    ⅛ tsp paprika
    ⅛ tsp cayenne pepper
    Water (less than ¼ c)
    2 inches vegetable oil in a pan

    Topping
    1 oz mozzarella
    1 Roma tomato, chopped
    2 Tbs sour cream
    ¼ C fresh cilantro, chopped
    1 Tbs milk
    ⅛ tsp salt

Mix the first six ingredients and add just enough water so it becomes a stiff dough. If necessary add a little more chickpea flour, and form into a cylinder with your hands. Slide it into your press. There is no need to oil it, your hands, or anything. Now heat your oil in the pan. To test, take a tiny bit of the dough and put it in the hot oil. See if it floats up. If it sinks and no bubbles form, the oil is not hot enough. If it browns quickly, it's too hot. Adjust heat accordingly. Then put the plunger in your extruder and turn the crank directly over the oil, filling the whole pan with noodles. With a pair of metal skewers, start turning them over. Cook on both sides about 5 minutes or until golden. Remove with a slotted spoon or strainer, and place on paper towels to cool.

   Arrange the noodles on a baking sheet covered with tinfoil ,and sprinkle on the cheese and the chopped tomato. Place in a toaster oven at 350°F until the cheese is melted. While that is heating, mix the sour cream, chopped cilantro, and salt, and thin with milk until the mixture is pourable. Take the nachos out of the oven and drizzle with the sour cream mixture. Be forewarned: it's awfully messy, but there's no other way to eat it but with your fingers. Maybe this should be called Garbanzo Fideo Chaat?

Sev Nachos

CREAM OF WHEAT FRITTERS

My mother was a child of the Great Depression. It had a permanent impact on her relationship with food: simply that there must always be a lot of it. It didn't need to be good, just as long as there was more food than anyone could possibly eat. Even after my siblings and I grew up and moved away, she kept a second freezer in the garage filled with stale bread, which she insisted was "just like fresh." Of course it was not. When I began to show interest in cooking, she loved telling me about the food of her childhood. Her mother, who died before I was born, would buy unplucked chickens to save a few cents, and often brought lice into the house, too. She cooked all manner of organ meats, including lung, which at the time had not yet been declared "unfit for human consumption" by the United States Department of Agriculture . Naturally, I hunted down all these odd ingredients wherever they could be found and agreed that they were all delicious. Wasn't it a shame that no one, in particular my father, wanted to eat them anymore?

One ingredient, however, I recall her describing in the fondest terms:

cream of wheat. Not just cooked, but sliced and fried and served for breakfast. I had never tasted it; in fact, developing this recipe was my very first experience with it. I had never even noticed it in the supermarket, but there it was, on the bottom shelf, below the trendy steel-cut oats.

Cream of Wheat has a strange history. There is, of course, Rastus. As I was writing this book, the manufacturer assured everyone that the grinning Black servant man holding a steaming bowl of cereal would be gone, along with Aunt Jemima and Uncle Ben. Despite their efforts to rehabilitate the image, it remains racist all the same, perpetuating stereotypes that go back more than a century. Nonetheless, in early 2021, his face is still on the boxes at my grocery. Maybe they don't move too quickly.

Then there is the origin story of the cereal itself, apparently entailing what is called *middlings*, a by-product of milling wheat. It was marketed to customers with the cheery jingle "Cream of Wheat Is So Good to Eat You Can Eat It Every Day . . . It's good for growing babies . . ." or something to that effect. My parents sang it all the time. But we never had the cereal growing up.

So I bought a box of it, cooked it and chilled it, sliced and fried it. I was expecting it to be crunchy like leftover polenta. Nope. It's soft, and very tasty, comforting and cozy. It reminds me of French toast and would be good just drizzled with maple syrup. I am not a product of the Depression, however. I was raised in an era of gastronomic depravity on Doritos and Cheez Doodles. I simply had to desecrate this product. And let me tell you, a little saltiness, some sour, some burn on the tongue, something creamy. It was overkill, but I could see these having been served at an ostentatious disco party in the 1970s.

3 packs or 1 C Cream of Wheat (or other brand of farina)
1 ½ C milk
Grating nutmeg
½ tsp salt
1 Tbs butter
Umeboshi paste
Kewpie mayo
Grainy mustard
Marmite
Hardboiled egg
Black lumpfish caviar

There are different kinds of Cream of Wheat requiring different cooking times. I used the Instant that comes in individual packs. It involved simply pouring the pack into a bowl with milk and salt, and microwaving for 1 ½ minutes. Grate in a little nutmeg and pour the cereal into a rectangular plastic container and let chill overnight.

The next day, turn out the solid rectangle onto your cutting board, slice into about 8 or 10 pieces, and fry them gently in the butter, turning them over to brown on both sides. Then arrange on a plate and add whatever you have in the fridge that will squirt or look wildly decorative. I came up with the ingredients listed above, but anything is fine as long as you get a nice blast of flavor and don't make a complete mess. Well, of course you can, if that makes you happy!

Cream of Wheat Fritters

Bowls

Salads, Pasta, Soups, Rice, and Grains

LEFTOVER TRI-TIP

Whatever I cook, there is always some left over. It's not that I can't judge how much will be eaten, it's that I like having little bits to experiment with the next day. Moreover, I never double a recipe so I can eat the same thing the next day; I just make a little extra, of everything. Steaks are always too big for one meal, so is a whole cut-up chicken, so is a pan full of sautéed vegetables. Think of this as the base for tomorrow's nosh, not to be eaten cold, but simply warmed up and placed in an entirely different context. Anything can go into a soup, made with stock you have in the freezer, a few vegetables, slices of meat, and some noodles. Even those can be leftovers. Stray bits of ingredients can also be placed in an omelet, jumbled together on a tortilla, or rolled in a rice paper wrapper. Or throw some tortilla chips into a pan with tomatoes, beans, and other leftovers for an improvised version of chilaquiles. This is why you should always cook too much.

 The easiest use of leftovers is to heat them and put them on toast or a bun. Let me offer a few examples of the latter.

1 small beef tri-tip
1 tsp salt
Spice rub including thyme, paprika, oregano, cumin, mace, fenugreek, garlic powder
1 tsp olive oil
1 tsp balsamic vinegar

1 Tbs butter
1 tsp smoked chipotle hot sauce
1 pretzel roll
½ tsp Dijon mustard
½ tsp horseradish
Aged cheddar cheese (such as Fiscalini) for grating

Tri-tip is one of the more common cuts found in California, a triangular bottom sirloin cut. Flank steak or skirt will work fine, too. To start, poke a small paring knife into the steak all over, on both sides, intentionally across the grain, which appears to run in different directions on both sides. This tenderizes the meat and allows the marinade to seep in. Rub the meat with the salt and spices. The combination of spices isn't as important as putting on a lot. Place the meat in a sealable plastic bag and pour over the oil and vinegar. Let marinate at least 1 hour. Then grill over a very hot flame, 10 minutes each side for rare. Let rest 10 minutes or longer, and slice thinly. Serve for dinner, ideally as a Santa Maria barbecue with pinquito beans and a big salad.

The next day, take 3 or 4 slices of leftover tri-tip and cut them into thin strips. Reheat them in the butter and add the hot sauce. While that's heating, divide and toast a pretzel roll and spread one side with mustard and the other with horseradish. Pile on the tri-tip, along with the juices, and grate a riot of cheese over the top while still hot so it melts. If it goes all over the place, great. In flavor it's sort of like a cheese steak, and in fact if I were in Philadelphia, I might even try making this with a real soft pretzel. Doesn't that sound wonderfully messy?

Leftover Tri-Tip

LEFTOVERS IN MINESTRONE

Pasta is served at my house at least once or twice a week. And there is almost always some leftover noodles and sauce, kept separately in plastic containers, waiting in the fridge until the next morning. Sauced noodles will not survive, alas. Ideally, you want a small shape that can be scooped up with a spoon, maybe ditalini or macaroni or little pennette. There can be no measurements for this recipe, not only because breaking out measuring cups is sometimes odious, but also because there is no way of assuring your leftovers will be in any particular measure, and most important, it doesn't matter. If you can get all the ingredients in roughly equal proportions, then proceed.

Soffritto
1 celery stalk, diced finely
1 carrot, diced finely
1 small onion or large shallot, diced finely
Olive oil
Pinch of salt

The Soup
1 bay leaf
1 Roma tomato, chopped
2 C stock
Pasta
Leftover meat and vegetables

Start with a simple soffritto, adding the celery, carrot, and onion or shallot to a pot, and cook gently with olive oil and a pinch of salt. Then make the soup. Add 1 fresh bay leaf. I know there are those who scorn the leaf, believing it has no flavor. The ones that are sold dry in jars left sitting on the shelves for a few years are flavorless, but a fresh leaf is lovely. To this add the tomato. Add to this about 2 cups of stock. If you have your own, fabulous, but if not, there are some good concentrated stocks, such as Better Than Bouillon. Absolutely any flavor will also work. Chicken is the most common, or beef, but fish stock is great in this soup, as is a shellfish stock made from leftover shrimp, crab, or lobster shells.

Any kind of leftover vegetable can go in, but beans are especially good. You can also throw in raw little broccoli florets, cauliflower, or some sliced cabbage. Little meatballs are great, but so is fish if you are going in that direction. In fact, if you don't have a leftover protein, add one in raw. Just slice it thinly, add a little salt, dust with cornstarch, and slip in the pieces in the last few minutes of cooking. That's the same time you should add your leftover pasta. You can actually throw uncooked pasta in, too; it just takes a little longer, and you might have to add hot water because it will soak up the broth. On a cold day, this is so very satisfying.

MUNG BEAN NOODLE SALAD

When it gets hot out, you want food that is not only cool temperature-wise, but also something light and cooling—something sour that refreshes and quenches thirst and hunger. A riot of raw vegetables sure is nice, especially over something more substantial and quick. Cold noodles do the trick. You might remember those pasta salads of the 1980s laden with cheese, cured meat, and thick noodles drenched in dressing. I loved them. But imagine exactly the opposite, and you will get the vibe of this dish.

1 handful (about 2 oz) mung bean threads, vermicelli, or saifun
3 Tbs soy sauce
1 small knob of ginger
1 Tbs tamarind paste
2 Tbs toasted sesame oil

1 small purple carrot, sliced
1 small orange carrot, sliced
1 handful bean sprouts
6 small cherry tomatoes, halved
½ avocado, sliced
Few sprigs of cilantro
1 lime
2 Tbs olive oil
Pinch of salt

Cover the mung bean threads with boiling water and let sit for 20 minutes. Drain but do not rinse, then put in a large bowl. While still hot, pour the soy sauce over the noodles. Grate the ginger and squeeze out the juice and add that, too. Discard the ginger solids. Dissolve the lump of tamarind paste in a half-cup hot water, and strain, to remove the seeds and inner fibers. Add the resulting liquid. Stir and add the sesame oil. Place in the fridge until the next day, covered, so well chilled.

On top of the noodles add the carrots, sprouts, cherry tomatoes, and avocado. Cover with cilantro and squeeze in the lime, drizzle with olive oil, and add a pinch of salt if you think it needs it. Eat with chopsticks.

RICE

My grandmother cooked. That's just about all she did. Frying onions, cutting up chickens, rolling out dough with her bulbous arms swaying back and forth, cigarette dangling from her mouth. I would sit on a red stool in her kitchen watching her. It never occurred to me to ask her to write anything down.

When I was young, she came to stay with us for two weeks while my parents made their first trip to Europe. Grandma cooked for me and my older brother and sister, but one night she decided to take us all to the grand buffet at the American Hotel in Freehold, New Jersey. It was an early nineteenth-century building adorned with horsey prints and lawn jockeys, in homage to the Raceway, a few blocks away. Richard Caton Woodville painted the front porch as it appeared in 1848 as the news of the Mexican War reached New Jersey. That painting and the sign over the porch both hung in the hotel vestibule.

This was the early 1970s, when the word "buffet" had not yet been tarnished by association with its worst iterations. There were mountains of food, but it was classy. You dressed up because it was a special occasion and quite elegant. Huge roasts of beef and lamb, shellfish, lasagna. There were dozens of dishes kept warm over Sterno burners. For reasons that now elude me, all I wanted was rice.

"The time I took my grandson to a buffet and all he ate was rice" became a story she loved to tell to relatives, friends, random passers-by. "Can you believe it, just rice!?" It was the most absurd situation she could imagine, not because it was a waste of money (which it was), but because I could have gorged myself on any number of delicious dishes, but only wanted white rice.

Rice remains one of my favorite foods, comforting in its utter simplicity. Any type of rice does the trick, too: risotto, sticky rice, jasmine, basmati. So I try to cook rice at least once a week, and I always make enough for leftovers. The trick is to freeze single-cup portions in Ziploc bags while still warm. Then pop them in the microwave for exactly one minute. A bowl of steaming koshihikari with a raw egg stirred in is about as good as a nosh gets. But here are a few things for more elaborate dishes, all quick and fabulous.

To Cook Rice
Pour 2 cups of basmati rice in a pot, rinse in water, swirl with your hand and pour it out; repeat several times until no longer cloudy. Cover with water and then put your index finger in the pot touching the top of the rice. Pour in

more water until it comes just above your fingernail and up to the first bend in your finger. Add a pinch of salt, and bring to the boil. Immediately turn down the heat and let simmer gently for 20 minutes. Turn off the heat and let rest for a further 10 minutes. Fluff with a fork. Eat half and put the other 2 cups into Ziploc bags in the freezer.

A rice cooker, incidentally, is a wonderful thing. I own an absurdly expensive enameled cast iron device, made by Vermicular, that makes rice better than I do. But it takes an hour, including a soaking cycle. There are many cheaper and excellent models out there too. Zojirushi is legendary.

KEDGEREE

1 egg
¼ onion
1 Tbs butter
1 small filet smoked trout or haddock
1 C cooked basmati

½ tsp Madras curry powder
2 Tbs heavy cream
1 lemon
5 or 6 sprigs of cilantro or parsley, chopped

Put the egg in a small pot and boil for 4 minutes. While that's boiling, chop the onion and fry it in the butter, but don't let it brown. While that's frying, skin and flake the fish. Remove the egg from the heat and rinse under cold water. Add the cooked rice to the frying onion, and then add the fish. Sprinkle in the curry powder and pour in the cream. Serve garnished with lemon wedges and cilantro.

Variations abound. Instead of adding curry powder, use soy sauce and ginger. It's very different from fried rice, but equally good. Fish sauce and lime, with a squirt of sriracha, also works beautifully in this recipe, especially if you have jasmine rice in the freezer. I have also used Worcestershire sauce and Tabasco. In fact, rice seems to be amenable to any combination of condiments.

Kedgeree

ZŌSUI

In Japan, it is common to eat leftover rice in a kind of soup mixed with other ingredients, called zōsui. I prefer it arranged in a bowl so that I can taste the individual ingredients, and appreciate the rifts, valleys, and contrasts of color that should reflect the season. Any leftovers can go in, and any soup base—but I think the soup should be just enough to moisten rather than drown the contents. Here I went in two entirely different directions. As for the rice, keep leftovers in sealable plastic bags. Pop one in the microwave for 60 seconds, and it's great.

#1

½ C Japanese rice
2 cremini mushrooms
1 tsp butter
⅛ tsp sea salt
Small handful chopped napa cabbage
1 small piece barbecued eel
3 pieces kamaboko
1 C dashi stock
1 scallion

Put the hot rice in the center of a small bowl. Slice the mushrooms and cook quickly in butter and salt. Arrange the mushrooms next to the rice, then cook the cabbage in the same pan, and add to the bowl. Add the eel and shave three pieces of kamaboko with a vegetable peeler, curl them up, and add to the bowl. Pour over the hot stock and garnish with the scallion, chopped.

#2

½ C Japanese rice
2 cremini mushrooms
1 tsp butter
⅛ tsp salt
Small handful of napa cabbage, chopped
Shreds of smoked turkey ham
1 small piece leftover breaded chicken breast
1 C rich chicken stock
Sprig of dill

Proceed exactly as above, but using the chicken and turkey instead.

Zosui

FETTUCCINE FOR CHRISTMAS

Fresh noodles to nosh on? I just happened to have made this on Christmas day, when off from work, hence the name. It's good exercise too. If you are inclined to meditate with a wad of dough on a wooden board rather than stretch your limbs on a yoga mat, then you will be enlightened gastronomically. Let me also assure you that this dish can be made with dried noodles and it's still very good. The noodling takes a little practice, but as I have been arguing for a long time, it is simple and even children can do it on the first go.

Turkey Ham
1 huge turkey leg
1 Tbs salt
1 tsp sugar
¼ tsp Insta Cure #1
Pinch each ground pepper, cloves, cinnamon, nutmeg, chili, and whatever else you like

Dough
1 C all-purpose flour, plus extra for dusting
1 jumbo egg
¼ tsp salt

Other Ingredients
2 Tbs salted butter
2 sprigs fresh thyme
¼ C crushed walnuts
½ C port wine
½ C Stilton cheese
1 scallion

Start by curing the turkey in a heavy plastic bag, mixing the "Turkey Ham" ingredients well. Place in the fridge and turn over every day or so for a week. Then bake the leg for an hour at 350°F. Place in the fridge overnight, and then slice off the bone, discarding the skin, tendons, and bones. Set aside ½ cup for this recipe, and cut into small pieces.

When you are ready, make the dough: In a large bowl with a fork, mix the flour, egg, and salt. Then get your hands into it, forming a smooth ball, and knead on a wooden board for about 5 minutes until smooth. Let rest a few minutes, flour your board well, and roll out the dough as thinly as you can, trimming off the edges if they become ragged. This dough should cover a 14″ × 20″ board. Don't worry about adding too much flour, if it sticks. This isn't pie dough; all the flour will get cooked. You just don't want it bone dry so that it cracks. Then, using a sharp knife, cut the dough into long strips. If you like them wider, that's fine. If you have the patience to make them narrower, great. Get a pot of water boiling with a pinch of salt. Put in the noodles. Cooking will take about 3 minutes. In that time, proceed immediately to the next step.

Melt the butter in a pan, and add the thyme and walnuts. Using a pair of tongs, transfer the noodles directly from pot to pan without rinsing. Let them sizzle together for a minute, then add the port, tossing the pan to distribute the ingredients. Pour out onto a plate and sprinkle on the Stilton and a little chopped scallion. Serve immediately. This dish feeds two people—or one, if you're really greedy! It looks very nice on a plate, but I am inclined to put it in a bowl and use chopsticks.

Fettuccine for Christmas

BACALAO À LA VIZCAINA

This is a traditional dish from Spain, also very popular in Mexico and Puerto Rico, especially for Christmas Eve. Vigils of holy days were times of fasting, when no meat or dairy products could be consumed. The idea was that meat is very nourishing and would stimulate the libido. Fish, being cold and moist, along with vegetables, is exactly the opposite and would help people maintain their penitential behavior. I haven't messed much with this dish and have just used slightly different ingredients so they remain distinct. A hard-boiled egg is also traditional, but I don't think it's necessary.

1 small skinless filet (about 4 oz) salt cod
10 tiny red, white, and purple potatoes
2 Tbs olive oil
2 cloves garlic, peeled and thinly sliced
4 large Cerignola olives
¼ C raisins
4 sundried tomatoes, cut in large pieces, in olive oil
1 C white wine
2 Tbs pasilla sauce

Soak the cod in water for 24 hours, changing the water often. Then fry the potatoes whole in the olive oil over low heat for about 15 minutes, turning them over every now and then. While that's happening, make your pasilla sauce: soak the split and seeded pasilla negro chili in boiling water for 10 minutes and blend into a fine puree. Set aside. Add the garlic to the pan. Toss everything around so it cooks through, without browning. After a few minutes, cut the fish into cubes and add it to the pan. Cut the olive flesh off the pit and add that; then the raisins and the tomatoes, with their oil. Add in the wine and the pasilla sauce. Cook over low heat without stirring for about 15 minutes until everything comes together. Just stir together at the last minute. You don't want the fish or potatoes to fall apart or get mushy. Just serve this on a plate or in a bowl.

Bacalao à la Vizcaina

ANCIENT GRAINS

On a cold day, a warm bowl of steaming grains, held between your hands and scooped with a favorite spoon, is comfort and joy. Oatmeal has its passionate devotees, and when it comes to whole oats cooked in broth rather than sweetened, I concur enthusiastically. But there are so many other fabulous grains that deserve our affection. Here are a few, each cooked in its own way. As with every recipe in this book, you can take the long, arduous method from scratch or use store-bought ingredients. I keep containers of homemade stock in the freezer just for cooking, but jarred concentrate is admittedly quicker—and I always have a few bases on hand, too. They come in a dazzling array of flavors these days.

The first is made from millet, which is among the most ancient of domesticated crops. The earliest archaeological remains of noodles were fashioned from millet, found in China, in a bowl that was overturned in an earthquake thousands of years ago. Millet was actually more important than rice in Asia at the time. It was used by the ancient Romans in their porridge, which was also made with barley or spelt—the ancestor of polenta long before corn arrived from the Americas. How it ever became relegated to the bird feeder rather than the bowl, I cannot imagine. The second recipe uses cracked buckwheat, which is apparently not a grain at all, but a relative of rhubarb. This is a riff on the Eastern European kasha. Finally, there is the tiny and utterly exquisite grain from West Africa called fonio, which was almost entirely unheard of outside that region until recently. I've tried to match the ingredients and garnishes in an interesting way, but use what you prefer to perk up your bowl.

MILLET POLENTA

2 C water	1 tsp Chile Crunch
1 tsp salt	1 tsp sunflower seeds
1 C whole millet	1 tsp fresh ginger, grated
1 C coconut milk	½ tsp grated palm sugar
1 scallion, chopped	

This is cooked exactly as you would make corn polenta. Boil 2 cups of water with salt. Then slowly pour in the millet by hand, and with a large wooden spoon, stir with the other hand. Then lower the heat and let it cook about 10 minutes. When the grain has absorbed most of the liquid, add ¾ of the coconut milk and stir again. Let continue cooking until soft and thickened, about another 20 minutes. Pour into a bowl and garnish with the other ingredients and the final bit of coconut milk.

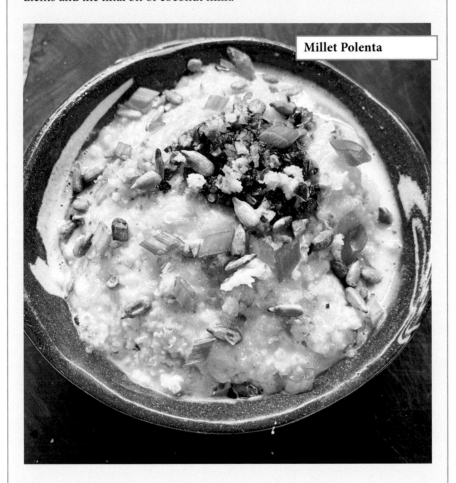

Millet Polenta

BUCKWHEAT OR KASHA BOWL

2½ C goose stock (or turkey or chicken)
1 C medium-ground buckwheat
1 egg
1 Tbs goose fat
½ C kale
½ C goose leg meat

This is one instance where you may choose to make stock or use store-bought. For the former, salt and season a goose with herbs such as thyme, dill, and fennel. Poke it all over with a skewer so the fat renders. Then roast it in a large baking pan for about 2 ½ hours at 350°F. Let rest at least half an hour. Save the fat. Remove the meat from the bones. Put all the bones, giblets, and wings in a large stockpot, cover with water, and add 1 tablespoon of salt, 2 ribs of celery, sprigs of thyme, and an onion. Simmer covered for 12 hours, preferably overnight. In the morning strain into a smaller pot and gently reduce by half for about an hour or longer. Pour into plastic containers and let cool, then move to the freezer. You can do this with leftover turkey carcass from Thanksgiving or chicken bones you've saved in the freezer. When you're ready to nosh, just bring a small pot of stock to the boil.

Mix the buckwheat with the egg and then cook in a heated pan (with no oil) until the grains are all separate and toasty. Then pour the grain into the pot of stock and simmer about 15–20 minutes, until cooked through. While that's happening, remove the stems from the kale and chop coarsely, then melt the goose fat (which was rendered from the roasted goose), cook the kale in the fat, and warm the goose meat. Pour half the kasha into a bowl and garnish with the kale and goose meat. Save the other half of the kasha in a plastic bag in the freezer, and for your next meal just microwave a few minutes to reheat.

FONIO

This is the quickest and easiest grain to cook, and it is utterly forgiving. If you find it a little dry, just add more liquid; it won't overcook. The brand most easily found in the United States is Yolélé, imported from Senegal.

    1 C fish broth
    ½ C fonio
    ¼ C tiny dried shrimp
    1 Tbs tamarind paste (from a block)
    ¼ C roasted peanuts, crushed

You can make a fish stock with bones in about 20 minutes, just simmered with a few aromatics, such as celery, onion, and carrot—or use a concentrate. In West Africa, it's common to use Maggi cubes, a kind of bouillon. I've even used dashi stock, which was quite delicate and perfumed.

Simply heat the stock, add the dried shrimp, and then add the fonio and let simmer on low for a minute. Then let rest covered for about 5 minutes until the liquid is absorbed. In the meantime, pour about 1 cup of boiling water over the tamarind, crush with a fork, and strain into a bowl. Scoop the fonio over the tamarind, and top with the crushed peanuts. The sourness of the tamarind goes perfectly with the saltiness of the fish and shrimp.

Now I encourage you to find any grain, such as whole wheat berries or farro, barley, kamut, emmer, or maybe even rye, wild rice, or steel-cut oats. The grain can be whole or cracked; the latter takes less time to cook. People often soak grains overnight or put them in an instant pot, which dramatically reduces the cooking time. And then garnish with your favorite vegetable, some fresh herbs, maybe a squirt of citrus, a pinch of chili pepper, and you can be happy knowing you are eating something eminently good-tasting and good for you.

Fonio

FRESH SEMOLINA NOODLE NESTS

I believe that noodle soup is the finest vehicle for pasta, but these little, crunchy nests have undeniable charm, especially topped with an egg and garnished lavishly. The contrasts in texture are really exciting. Remarkably, I got the idea from nineteenth-century Russian cookbook author Elena Molokhovets, who fills little timbales with fresh vermicelli, butter, and cheese.

1 C semolina flour
½ tsp salt
⅓–½ C water, plus another 3 C
1 Tbs butter
Eggs (1–2 per person)
¼ C pistachios, crushed
¼ barberries, soaked in hot water 10 minutes, and drained
¼ tsp dried mint

Put the flour and salt in a mixing bowl, and gradually add one-third of a cup of water. Squeeze the mixture with your fist until it begins to come together as a dough, adding a little more water if necessary. You want a very firm dough. Begin to knead the dough on a wooden board. Put the extra water into the mixing bowl. Every now and then, dip your hands into the extra water and scrape off the excess. Then continue kneading with slightly wet hands. Eventually you'll see the water go cloudy with starch. What you're doing is removing some of the starch to bring up the percentage of protein in the dough. You can also add a pinch of vital wheat gluten if you like; I often do. Knead for about 15 minutes, continuing to dunk your hands in the water. The dough will be rubbery in the end and smooth. Roll it out as thin as you can, flouring well with regular bread flour to prevent sticking. I use a tapered French rolling pin for this, rather than an American-style handled pin. It gives you greater force. Remember to flour well at every stage of rolling. Then roll up the dough and cut into super-thin noodles. Flour them well, and toss around to prevent sticking. Form them into 8 little nests.

Heat the butter in a tiny frying pan about the size of your nest, and drop in the fresh noodles. Cook over low heat until brown, then flip over, browning the other side. Then crack an egg directly over the noodles and let cook on low until set. If you're making several, then of course use a large pan and cook many at once, with more butter. To serve, garnish with the other ingredients and a little more salt. You may also want a sprinkle of cayenne or a squirt of lime.

DUMPLINGS

Unfortunately our use of the homely little word "dumpling," in English, disgusting if you think about it, is made even less appealing through imprecise usage. Two entirely unrelated species of comestible have been lumped together. What is properly termed a "stuffed noodle"—the glorious range of dim sum offerings, every ravioli and its cousins, kreplach and Turkish manti—is not a dumpling, and we should henceforth desist from referring to them as such. A proper dumpling is dumped in soup, and nothing more. It is much less complicated than a stuffed noodle and perhaps for that reason even more satisfying and well suited to noshing. When you have a decent broth that can be heated up, you are minutes from a wonderfully proper dumpling. Here are three variations on the theme.

Sourdough Goose-Fat Dumpling

For this you will need great stale sourdough bread, whizzed in the blender to a fine powder. I find the texture of the dumpling is better in the end if you add some coarse crumbs as well, in equal proportion. Any fat, including chicken, works well. Ideally, you will have gently poached a few whole cloves of garlic in a few cups of the fat for flavoring.

   1 C sourdough breadcrumbs
   ½ tsp salt
   ¼ tsp ground black pepper
   1 egg
   ½ tsp baking powder
   1 Tbs goose fat
   3 C clear goose or chicken broth

Mix all the ingredients, and let them meld overnight if you have the time. Gently squeeze the crumbs, but not too tightly, into 4 balls. If you need a little more liquid so they hold together, just add a tiny amount of water or stock. Heat up your broth, and when it is simmering, drop in the balls and let them cook about 10 minutes, covered. You can garnish the soup with a few leaves of cabbage and some scallions, cooked with the dumplings. And if you're feeling extravagant, add some paprika and a dollop of sour cream, but it's awfully good unadorned as well.

Sourdough Goose-Fat Dumpling

Gnocchi

People look for light, evanescent gnocchi and rightly worry about overworking the dough so they become tough and too chewy. The solution? Don't use wheat flour. And then, who has the time to cook potatoes? The solution: use the microwave. This recipe really can be made in 10 minutes. A ricer is the key to light and fluffy texture ,too.

    1 russet potato about the length of your hand
    1 tsp salt
    ¼ C oat flour
    1 egg yolk
    1 Tbs butter
    1 Tbs Gruyère cheese, grated
    ¼ tsp nutmeg, grated

Microwave the potato on high for 5 minutes. Start a small pot of salted water boiling. When the potato is done, cut it in half and place it face down in the ricer, peel and all, and force it through the holes. Do the same with the other half, and then stir around the peels and press again to get every last bit of potato. You should have about a cup of fluffy potato. Sprinkle it with the oat flour and let cool a minute or so. Then add the egg yolk. Knead just until it comes together. Pinch off little bits the size of a large marble and roll over a ridged gnocchi paddle or over the back of a fork. You should have about 16 gnocchi. Place in the boiling water for 2 minutes, then scoop them out directly into a pan of butter. Sprinkle with the grated cheese until it all emulsifies and serve. Grate the nutmeg right on top at the last minute.

Serviettenknödel

I once taught a historic cooking class in Vienna and met up with my old friend Mike, who was living there. He took me to a very traditional little hole-in-the-wall restaurant, and I ate only things that upset him, such as a lung stew and a kind of dumpling he told me not to order. So I had to. It was sort of like a soft, wet Wonder Bread, cooked in a napkin, I was told. It was tasty but nothing remarkable. Several years later I looked more closely at some recipes for the dish. It is not plain at all and is often made with serious bread and other delicious ingredients. I'm not sure that it counts as a proper dumpling, let alone a noodle. It is really a stuffing, steamed in a napkin. Sounds ordinary? I assure you that it is sublime. Especially after cooling and frying up for a glamorous nosh.

4 slices of ciabatta or other crusty bread, 1 inch thick
1 whole egg and one egg white
¾ C whole milk
2 Tbs melted butter
1 shallot, chopped
1 tsp salt
1 tsp paprika
½ tsp freshly ground pepper
½ C parsley, chopped
½ C smoked ham, finely diced
2 C beef broth
2 Tbs lard

Rip the bread into small pieces and soak with the eggs, milk, and butter a few minutes. Add all the other ingredients. Get a sturdy napkin or thin dishcloth.

Place the mixture inside and roll it up tightly. Tie the ends with string. Get a fairly tall pot and tie the ends of the rolled napkin to the handles on either side, so the sausage-shaped dumpling is suspended inside the pot but not touching the bottom. Add the beef broth and bring to the boil. Simmer for 30 minutes. Remove the dumpling and let cool a few minutes. You can slice it and serve it now. Or you can wrap it in plastic and put in the fridge a few hours. Then unwrap and slice it and fry in the lard, turning over often until crisp and browned. A few slices of this is all you need.

AMARANTH SUSHI

Some grains simply don't stick together well enough to hold together in a rolled sushi, but amaranth is an exception. The nutty flavor also goes so nicely with the fish that it doesn't need any further embellishment.

¾ C water	1 smoked trout filet
⅛ tsp salt	1 Tbs mayonnaise
½ C amaranth	2 sheets of nori

Bring the water to the boil in a small pot with the salt. Add the amaranth, and lower the heat. Simmer very gently, covered, for 20 minutes. Remove the lid, and let the steam rise in the hot pot, stirring now and then, until the amaranth is completely dry and cool. Mix the trout and mayonnaise. Pass the sheets of seaweed over an open flame for just a second so that they are toasty and crisp. Divide the amaranth between the two sheets, and make a thin layer. Place the trout in a thin line along the middle. Then place the whole thing in a sushi rolling mat, and roll up tightly, pressing it in with the edge of the mat rolled around it. Remove the whole roll, and very gently, so that you don't squish out the contents, cut into 4 parts with a serrated bread knife. Repeat with the other sheet. Makes 8 small pieces.

CARP QUENELLES IN SOUP

When my children were young, we won a goldfish at the California State Fair by tossing a ping-pong ball some distance into a glass of water. We named the goldfish Eurydice and brought her home in a plastic bag of water. Once at home the little fish was moved to a big, luxurious aquarium with mermaids and a treasure chest and a sunken ship half buried in the gravel. She was happy and enjoyed being sung to. I even got in the habit of petting her under the surface of the water.

Eurydice ate well. Who knew that goldfish like leftovers? Her favorites were sausage, spaghetti and meatballs, pancakes. I think she ate some foods just to please me. Of course she grew. And grew. And eventually seemed to fill the entire tank. She no longer looked like a little goldfish but more like a big carp or a slightly less than glamorous koi.

One day after I picked the boys up, we got home to find Eurydice on the floor. She had leaped to her demise, obviously seeking a bigger fishpond. For the briefest of seconds I thought of getting out a frying pan. Well, fish always taste of whatever they've been eating, right? I might have put that theory to the test. Instead, we laid her gently in the earth with Hades—perhaps she had looked back when trying to escape. Why we gave her that name, I shall never know.

I still can't cook carp without remembering her, or the dictum about fish tasting like what they eat. I've had carp that taste exactly like mud and garbage. Some taste sweet and have a delicate light flesh. There's no way to tell when you buy it, which is why I suspect people turn more readily to pike or perch or other freshwater fish. Think of quenelles de brochet, or gefilte fish. Any of these will work in this recipe. But if you still have a tender spot for your pet goldfish, try salmon, which is much easier to find.

This serves two, because it's much easier to poach in this proportion.

Cure for Fish
8 oz fish
1 tsp salt
1 sprig dill
1 tsp vodka

Choux Paste
¼ C water
1 ½ Tbs flour
1 egg
¼ C milk

3 C fish stock or dashi stock

Cut the fish into small cubes and add the other ingredients for the cure. Leave it in the fridge for a day or more. When ready to make the quenelles, bring your stock to a very gentle simmer. You can use fishbones and aromatics, such as carrot, celery, and onion, gently boiled for about 20 minutes and then strained, or simply use a store-bought fish stock to save time. Even Japanese dashi stock works well.

In a mortar, pound the fish for several minutes until it sticks together and becomes a solid mass. You could do this in a food processor, but I think a mortar is easier.

Then heat the water and flour in a small pot just until the butter is melted. Add the flour, and stir until it becomes a sticky ball of dough. Let cool a few minutes, and then add the egg, stirring in vigorously so it is completely mixed in. Add the milk, and stir that, too. Then add the fish, and beat it all together for a few minutes.

Using two wet tablespoons, form the fish paste into little torpedo shapes by scraping from one spoon to another. Drop them right from the spoon into the gently simmering stock. You'll get about 10 quenelles. In about 5 minutes they'll float to the top. Cook another 5 minutes, then serve. I like the simple elegance of this dish ungarnished. You can also chill these in the stock and serve cold with some horseradish or wasabi on the side.

Carp Quenelles in Soup

CEVICHE

There is really no recipe for this beyond the following advice. Find the freshest and most pleasantly aromatic fish possible. I found one-third of a pound of hamachi, or yellowfin tuna intended for sushi. Cut the fish into thin slices with a stainless steel knife. Carbon steel will actually affect the flavor. Squeeze a lime over the fish. Slice a shallot finely and add that, and a single green chili—a jalapeño or serrano if you like it hotter. Sprinkle with salt; for ⅓ lb of fish I used ½ teaspoon. Mix everything up. You can eat it immediately, after marinating for just a few minutes, or after an hour or so. Longer, and the texture and color of the fish change entirely. It will still be tasty, but completely cooked, in a sense, by the acid. Now, if you want to play with this a little, try wrapping it up in a rice paper wrapper with watercress. Or lay it flat on a plate as they used to do with tuna as a "carpaccio" and drizzle excellent olive oil on top. I have even set these ingredients in a fish aspic, which is much more delicious than it sounds—and the lime doesn't impede the gelatin from setting. Just use a good fish stock, not a preflavored sweet gelatin mix.

GALINHADA WITH MANIOC GRITS

I was once invited to speak in Brazil at a college in a neighborhood called Niterói across the bay from Rio de Janeiro. The students had just seized the campus in protest, set up barriers, and spray-painted slogans on every surface. I was assured my talk would go on nonetheless. The students were well spoken, charged with Marxist ideology, and I was asked excellent, thought-provoking questions. Of course, the talk was about food, and I was taken to a local cafeteria for lunch. There were maybe a dozen dishes on a buffet steam table, simple hearty stews like feijoada with black beans and farofa, which is made from toasted manioc flour. It was the best meal I had in a week of eating in fine restaurants in Rio. One particular deep-red chicken stew still haunts me. It was called galinhada and was very simple: onions and tomato, with I think just a hint of peanut. Here is a simplified version, accompanied by what is a very unconventional way to make farofa, but it is instant and very reminiscent of grits.

Chicken Stew
1 Tbs olive oil (or red palm oil)
1 leftover chicken thigh
1 shallot, sliced
1 serrano chili
1 Roma tomato
1 tomatillo
1 tsp smoked paprika
¼ tsp salt or more to taste
¼ tsp peanut butter

Grits
2 C water
½ C farinha de mandioca (toasted cassava flour, which you can find online)
¼ tsp salt
1 tsp butter

Garnish
Handful cilantro, chopped
½ lime

To start, boil the water for the grits. Heat the oil in a small pan. Red palm oil (*dende*) is fantastic if you can find it. Shred the leftover chicken, and add it to the pan. Save the skin and bone for stock. Add the shallot, and then the chili. When those are barely cooked through, add the tomato and tomatillo, both chopped. Then add the paprika and salt. Let this all come together over a gentle flame for about 5 minutes.

Then add the manioc flour to the water and stir. Add in the salt and butter. At the last minute, add the peanut butter to the stew. It should just lend a hint of peanut; more than a dab overwhelms the other ingredients. To serve, put the stew in a small bowl with the grits and garnish with cilantro and a few wedges of lime. If you like it hotter, add some incendiary little pickled green chilies called *cumari verde*.

Galinhada with Manioc Grits

SHELLFISH STEW ON COUSCOUS

I hesitate to call this gumbo, but it does share some of the signature flavorings and techniques. Whatever trepidation you have in mind about the time it takes to make this, dispel it presently. —this is a 10-minute prep. Use frozen shrimp and scallops, and if you can find lobster stock concentrate, you are good to go. If the latter cannot be found, don't despair. Just save all the shrimp and crab shells from dinners you have prepared until you have a big bagful frozen. Simmer those barely covered in water with a glug of white wine and onion, celery, bay leaf, and salt for 20 minutes and strain. That's your shellfish stock. Freeze it if you have extra.

    1 Tbs salted butter
    1 Tbs flour
    ½ C couscous
    5 shrimp
    5 scallops
    1 shallot
    1 stalk of celery
    1 jalapeño
    1 Roma tomato
    1 C shellfish stock

In a small skillet, melt the butter and add the flour, stirring over gentle heat to make a roux. Meanwhile, boil half a cup of water in a small pot. When it boils, add the couscous and a pinch of salt, and turn off the heat and let rest covered. The rest of the dish will be done by the time it's ready. Defrost the shellfish in water, and drain. While that's happening, chop the shallot, celery, and jalapeño, minus the seeds, and add them to the roux. Let cook a few minutes on low heat. Then chop the tomato and add it. Add the shellfish, then the stock, and let simmer another few minutes until thick. Put the couscous in a bowl and pour over the stew. That's it, maybe hit with a little lemon juice if you like, or some pickled lemon.

Shellfish Stew on Couscous

BACALHAU WITH KALE AND MI GORENG

As a historian, I like to imagine the random culinary combinations that must have occurred as colonial invaders ran out of provisions and were forced to use local ingredients. We know, for example, that Lewis and Clark ran out of food and ate the dogs before they turned to native plants, such as camas and bitterroot. Dutch traders restricted on the island of Deshima outside Nagasaki bought Japanese soy sauce, pickles, and katsuobushi but probably prepared them in very European ways. Imagine the first taco that held beef. This combination occurred to me while trying to imagine the Portuguese with their salted, dried cod, adding it to the noodles they encountered in what is now Indonesia. The noodles themselves were introduced by Chinese traders, so it's actually a much more complicated mash-up. If you happen to see what is deceptively labeled as "Portuguese-style cod" in a small can, buy it. It's real bacalhau and saves days of soaking and cooking. The ramen is another serious convenience, easily found in an Asian grocery but prepared like Japanese ramen.

1 pack instant Mi Goreng–flavored ramen noodles
Extra black rice ramen noodles for contrast
4–5 small leaves of kale
1 can bacalhau

Boil the noodles according to package directions. Remove and discard the ribs from the kale, chop the leaves, and add right to the pot. Drain both, and add the flavoring packets and the drained fish. Mix thoroughly. You can also cook some thin, yellow wheat noodles, fry them with shallots, and add *kecap manis*, a kind of sweet soy sauce, and add fish you've soaked yourself for 24 hours. A bit of lime, and you're good to go.

Bacalhau with Kale and Mi Goreng

* * * * *

I hope that I have shown you that a great nosh need not come out of a bag purchased at the grocery store. It can be fresh, exciting, and even opulent. And most important, it can be enjoyed any time of day or night, on your own or with others. Make the most of life and nosh with conviction!

Glossary

æbleskiver Little round pancakes found in Scandinavia, as well as the pan in which they are cooked—a heavy metal pan with hemispherical depressions. The pan can be used for many other recipes, such as Japanese takoyaki with octopus, or even meatballs.

Branston Pickle English chutney-like condiment based vaguely on Indian prototypes. Brown, chunky, and sweet and sour, with vegetables such as rutabaga, onion, and carrot and apple and spices. Traditionally served with cheese but also goes beautifully on a sandwich.

brotform basket Basket woven from willow branches or other wood, round or oval, and used to let bread dough rise. It can be used bare and simply dusted with flour, which gives the bread a lovely ridged crust, or with a cloth inside, which gives a smooth surface.

bubble tea Black or green tea, or actually any beverage, served with tapioca starch balls (essentially pasta) floating within, drunk with a large straw through which one sucks up the chewy balls. Perversely pleasant. Originally from Taiwan, it became wildly popular in the United States in the 2010s and can still be found in most US cities and suburbs.

buttermilk powder An ingredient designed specifically for baking, this conveniently can be kept on the shelf and is ideal if you would rather not keep a carton of buttermilk in the refrigerator all the time. For the most part, you can just use regular buttermilk in the recipes here, without adjusting quantities, though for other baked goods you would want to reduce the volume of liquid proportionally.

cachaça Clear sugar-based alcohol, usually about 40 proof or more, from Brazil. Cachaça is something like rum, and is distilled from sugarcane juice. It originates from the time when sugarcane plantations were worked by enslaved African laborers and remains the signature alcohol of Brazil.

caipirinha Classic drink made from cachaça and lime juice. Ideally sipped slowly at the beach or poolside on a carefree afternoon, but also works perfectly fine with a nosh at any time of day.

chicharrónes A snack food of fried pig skins, when made well these are light and evanescent, perfectly crispy, without a greasy aftertaste, although they can include a sliver of fat and even meat. In the United States they are called pork rinds, in Britain scratchings. Some of the best come from the Philippines where they are flavored with garlic and vinegar.

Chile Crunch or Chili Crisp Brand names for a thick paste of chili, garlic, and oil that has now become generic. The original version is Chinese, called Lao Gan Ma, but there is also a milder Japanese version (S&B), another called Fly by Jing, and one made by David Chang of Momofuku. Undeniably among the most exquisite edible substances on earth.

cubeb Type of pepper from Indonesia that has a little spike or tail, more resiny and hotter than black pepper. Can be bought online and should be tried by anyone who loves complex heat.

dashi stock Staple in Japanese cuisine made from shavings of smoked and dried katsuobushi (skipjack tuna) though often with dried mackerel, or smaller fish, plus kombu seaweed. It is strained and clear, delicate, and when made well supplies the umami of glutamate in the seaweed with the inosinate of the fish, boosting the flavor of anything whose presence it graces. It is the base of miso soup and countless other dishes.

dukkah Egyptian condiment of ground nuts, such as hazelnuts or almonds, and spices, such as cumin, coriander, and pepper, plus herbs. It can be bought premade, but making your own in a mortar is easy, and you can add exactly what you like. Typically you dip bread first into olive oil, then into the dukkah. Dukkah is also lovely sprinkled on vegetables or in a sandwich.

eau de vie Clear alcohol from France distilled from grapes or any other fruit, such as raspberries, pears, or plums. It means "water of life," which is exactly what alcohol was believed to be in the late Middle Ages.

furikake Crushed nori seaweed flakes sprinkled on food, especially rice, at the last minute to add umami punch. There are dozens of different varieties. My favorite includes katsuobushi (tuna) flakes, dehydrated egg, and sesame seeds. Those with shiso (perilla) leaves or dried salmon are also excellent.

gochujang Fermented bean and chili sauce from Korea made with salt, inoculated glutinous rice, and barley malt. Usually aged in a large clay vessel until it becomes sweet, salty, and spicy. Improves the flavor of practically everything.

grains of paradise (melegueta pepper) More closely related to cardamom than to true pepper, this is a spice from the West Coast of Africa, piquant, alluringly nutty, fragrant. It was a star in medieval European cooking, but largely lost in the early modern period. It deserves a serious revival and can nowadays be bought online easily.

grappa Clear alcohol distilled normally from the leftover grape skins from wine making. It was originally an inexpensive way to get the most from a harvest, but now grappa can be a very expensive and refined product.

Halloumi Salty, fairly hard, goat and sheep milk cheese from the Middle East, specifically Cyprus, that grills or fries beautifully without melting.

HP Sauce A thick, brown sweet and sour sauce with an image of the English Houses of Parliament on the label. Similar to American steak sauce, but often eaten with a full English breakfast. The sourness comes from tamarind and tomatoes.

kamaboko A fish cake made by pulverizing white fish and rice starch, and then steaming a half-cylinder shape on a small slab of cedar or other wood. The texture is delightfully chewy. It is usually sliced and added to soup but can be used in myriad ways.

katsu sauce (tonkatsu sauce) A kind of sweet barbecue sauce made with dates and apples, similar to HP Sauce or A.1. Steak Sauce. In Japan it is meant to accompany fried breaded pork cutlets. Bulldog is the best-known brand, although there are other very nice ones. A quite similar okonomiyaki sauce is used with mayonnaise on the sumptuous pancake of the same name.

lime pickle Although there are many versions of this, the one I refer to here is from India and is extremely sour, salty, and a bit spicy. It contains garlic, ginger, fenugreek, chili, mustard seeds, and whole limes fermented. It is easy to make, but store-bought brands, such as Patak's and Mother's, can be excellent. It is eaten as a condiment with other foods but is also great in a sandwich.

lupin bean Although these beans contain a great amount of protein compared with other species , they are extremely bitter to start and never soften with cooking. Consequently, they need to be soaked and drained for several days, cooked, and then preserved in brine. The result is a little yellow oval that is salty, crunchy, and aesthetically more akin to the olive than to any other bean. To eat, remove the outer skin if you like and simply nibble as a snack.

Marmite Dark brown, extraordinarily salty sludge made from yeast that comes in a tiny jar and among Britons is spread on toast. It can also be used in cooking to great effect. Vegemite is an Australian version.

mirin Sweetened sake used in cooking. Feel free to use ordinary drinking sake and a little sugar, which I think is often much better than the standard supermarket mirin.

Mornay sauce Just a béchamel (flour and butter cooked together and thinned with milk) to which is added cheese. Gruyère is traditional, but any hard cheese that melts well will work. You can slather it on sandwiches, pour it over noodles (which is a curious dish called macaroni and cheese), or adorn your vegetables with it. It even makes a great topping for nachos or cheesy french fries.

nori Seaweed that is formed into a thin sheet, used to wrap sushi, but also crumbled for use as a garnish in Japanese cuisine and even eaten as a snack.

okonomiyaki Large Japanese pancake made with cabbage, grated nagaimo (mountain yam), pork belly or seafood, and other ingredients, even noodles in the layered Hiroshima version. The pancake is cooked on a large griddle with two big metal spatulas and topped with okonomiyaki sauce (which is similar to barbecue sauce), mayonnaise, and katsuobushi flakes.

passata Italian raw tomato puree without seeds or skins, bottled and pasteurized for preservation. The freshest form of tomato you can find without chopping ripe tomatoes. Mutti is an excellent brand, though there are others. I use it on pizza when I don't want a rich cooked taste, or in soups or stews.

pico de gallo "Rooster's beak" in Spanish. (Why? No one knows.) A fresh raw salsa made with coarsely chopped tomato, green onion, serrano chilies, salt, lime juice, and chopped cilantro. Practically all food is improved by such a garnish, especially if you use plenty of lime.

shichimi togarashi Chili powder from Japan that traditionally includes seven ingredients, though in practice often more, such as orange peel, black sesame seeds, sansho (green spice powder that numbs your tongue, similar to what Sichuan peppercorns do), ginger, seaweed, or poppy seeds. Sprinkled on soup or noodles, it adds a fiery and complex kick.

sodium citrate Chemical used to prevent cheese from separating when heated. It explains why products like Cheez Whiz and Velveeta are eminently meltable. It can be ordered online, and you only use a tiny amount for effect.

speck Smoked and cured ham, the best of which comes from the Tyrol in northern Italy, but similar products are found through much of the German-speaking world. It can be eaten thinly sliced and raw like prosciutto but is also cooked into other dishes.

surimi What is commonly called "imitation crab legs" in the United States, but is usually made from pollack or other whitefish, pulverized into a batter, spread in sheets. and rolled over itself to approximate the texture of flaky crab. In Japan, it is really not considered an imitation of anything, but rather a delicious ingredient in its own right.

tahdig In Persian cuisine, the crunchy bottom of rice cooked in a pan. Similar to the socarrat beloved in the bottom of a paella, and probably historically linked though the Moorish rule of Spain after 711.

tahini sauce Made of ground sesame seeds, tahini is used in hummus and the like. Mix it with lemon juice, salt, garlic, and a little water to thin it out, and you have a great sauce. I often make a simple quick sauce by mixing tahini paste with yogurt. If you are really adventurous, think of using tahini in the way we use peanut butter: spread it on a sandwich, mix it into a stew. It's even great in cookies.

Tajín Brand name of a salty lime- and chili-flavored powder from Mexico. Often put on mangos or other fruit, it can be used to perk up anything at the last minute before serving. Be careful, because if you use it regularly, nothing tastes quite right without it.

tamago pan Rectangular, often nonstick pan used for making tamagoyaki, which is a rolled scrambled egg popular in Japan and often said to be the true test of a restaurant because it is so simple. It is flavored with dashi stock and perhaps a touch of sugar, and (unlike an omelet) is made by cooking a small amount of egg at a time and rolling each layer carefully in the pan until it makes a wide, rolled-up egg.

tawa Traditional Indian pan for cooking flatbreads and dosas. It can be cast iron or nonstick, but a soapstone tawa is really remarkable. It needs to be cured with fat, like iron pans, but then becomes nonstick and holds heat a very long time. A Mexican clay or metal comal can be used as a substitute.

Taylor pork roll, Taylor ham Although the name is disputed, dividing those from southern and northern New Jersey, respectively, clearly anyone calling this "ham" is inaccurate. It is a wide, ground pork smoked sausage, nothing like ham. It is sliced into quarter-inch rounds and fried, then eaten on a roll with mustard for lunch or even for breakfast. It can be found outside the state if you are intrepid.

teff Small grain (*Eragrostis tef*) from Ethiopia, ground and made into the fermented flatbread injera.

umeboshi Small, soft red salted pickled fruits (ume). Though labeled plums, these fruits are actually in the apricot family. They are so intense that you really can't eat much. There is also a crunchy green variety (kari kari) that is well worth seeking out. They are used to add a little punch to rice or other dishes, and there is a paste in a jar or tube that is called for here for convenience.

yuzu Small green citrus from Japan. You can buy bottled yuzu juice as well as ponzu, which is also made from a citrus. Lime juice is okay as a substitute, though more sour, so use less.

zaʾatar Both an herb in the genus Origanum (oregano) and a spice mix containing other herbs, such as wild thyme and savory, plus ground sumac and sesame seeds. Found throughout the Middle East, but many people prefer the bright green Lebanese blend. Brush flatbread with oil and sprinkle with zaʾatar; rub a chicken with it before roasting; or generously dust cauliflower with it.

Index